I say nothing to him
I love him

Father Jacques

I SAY NOTHING TO HIM I LOVE HIM

Contemplative Prayer

Translated from the French
by
Florestine Audette, R.J.M.

MÉDIASPAUL

Médiaspaul benefits from The Canada Council for the Arts and SODEC Book Publishing Support Program.

Originally published as *Je ne lui dis rien, je l'aime: la prière contemplative*, by Éditions Bellarmin, Montreal, 1999.

Canadian Cataloguing in Publication Data

Jacques, père, 1952-

I say nothing to him, I love him: Contemplative prayer

Translation of: Je ne lui dis rien, je l'aime.
Includes bibliographical references.

ISBN 2-89420-456-6

1. Contemplation. 2. Prayer. 3. God — Worship and love. I. Title.

BV5091.C7J3213 2001 248.3'4 C2001-940216-3

Phototypesetting: *Médiaspaul*

Cover: *Summum Grafix Studio*

ISBN 2-89420-456-6

Legal Deposit — 2nd Quarter 2001
Bibliothèque nationale du Québec
National Library of Canada

250, boul. St-François Nord
Sherbrooke, QC, J1E 2B9 (Canada)
www.mediaspaul.qc.ca
libmedia@qc.aira.com

To those
who enlightened me
when they came to me
for advice.

Acknowledgements

I would like to express my thanks to Mr. Paul Longpré and to Lise, his wife. They agreed to read my manuscript and made a number of helpful suggestions for improving it. Their corrections were as numerous as they were beneficial to this work.

I also thank my community at Rougemont. Especially my Father Abbot, Dom André, who allowed me to pursue this work, Fr. Michel, who solved my difficulties with the computer, and Fr. Thomas for reading my text.

TABLE OF CONTENTS

Prologue
(in the form of a fable)

Once upon a time, all the animals held a large assembly. This was a long, long time ago. In fact, this occurred on the sixth day of creation, at about the noon hour. Birds and fish had been created the day before and, that very morning, the animals of the earth. All of them were absolutely astounded by such a profusion of colors and shapes. The Lion who, for the time being, ate only grass, but who was already making claims to royalty, convened all his subjects and held forth approximately as follows. (I say "approximately" for the exact words were not recorded. The good reason for this was that Adam was not there yet, God having deliberately set aside that very afternoon to make him.)

"Dear friends, everything is so splendid that before we spread out over all the earth, I think it would be proper for us to present an address to our Creator that would be worthy of him. This would be a first prayer, drafted by one of us in everyone's name."

Before he had finished his instructions, the Lion sensed that they would begin to think of him as their spokesperson. He hastened to add that his roar would not be in the required pitch and so it would be preferable to choose someone else.

The animals looked at one another. Their eyes gradually focused on the Parrot. He wore fine clothes and a bright plumage. He had a good beak and knew how to use it. Everyone had already noticed his eloquence, and since he had come into existence only the previous day, he was not yet known to be a great talker. Once he was chosen, he hastened to display his talent.

Very soon, the Lion found that the Parrot repeated himself.

"We would need someone more creative and more enlightened," he suggested.

The Monkey was pushed forward. He argued with great intelligence about God's five majestic dignities: two principal ones and three secondary ones.

He had hardly delivered three quarters of his speech when the Pink Flamingo, standing on one leg, fell asleep in spite of himself, his head tucked under his wing. This was a rhetorical failure. Another form of expression had to be found.

The Peacock knew he could argue in a different way. He took two steps forward, turned about and spread his tail. This was not done out of pride since original sin was not invented yet. Let us say that he wanted to make a fine presentation. The effect nonetheless was almost nil. The Hummingbird could do as well with much less ado.

Hoping to boost his candidacy, the Bear, who was never prone to be subtle, then insinuated out loud that in order to pray well one had to rise to the heights of God. The Giraffe, thinking they were talking about her, declared from on high:

"If it is a matter of hoisting oneself up to the level of the Listener, dear colleagues, kindly believe that I …"

The Elephant was already protesting with his two ears when the Fox, to save the situation, advised:

"You won't believe me, but I heard it said that He prefers little ones."

"But this is unbelievable!"

"Impossible. We would have to elect the Mosquito: we wouldn't even hear him …"

It is not that he could not make himself heard, but the Mosquito preferred to act without drawing too much attention. His strategy has hardly changed since then. He therefore declined the invitation.

The Giraffe had taken advantage of the confusion to conceal herself. The Crocodile, knowing what was coming, stole away, setting off the fact that he lacked the elegance needed for the occasion. The Vulture gave his trade as an excuse. The Hippopotamus, that he had teeth missing.

Right in the midst of this din, someone (exactly who was never known) suggested the Dog, because of his fidelity, recite a witty little encomium to God assuring him, for example, of everyone's attachment and loyalty. Ah! Most unfortunately for us, Humans, this suggestion had no support. If prayer had been given the Dog as its patron saint, perseverance would have been its main trait and the history of salvation would most likely have been altogether different. But tumult reigned.

When the uproar had calmed down somewhat, the Serpent, who was already crafty but not yet jealous since Eve did not exist, expressed the idea that, in his opinion, the Finch could satisfy everybody.

"Beautiful but without ostentation, elegant but not bombastic. With the reputation of being virtuous. Especially gifted with a lyricism capable of touching sensitive heartstrings. How well he would represent us with the rich high-soaring flights of his prayer! So many emotions, beautifully expressed and sung heartily! Surely God would be touched …"

They did not yet know that there is more joy in heaven for the prayer of publicans and sinners, that virtue therefore is superfluous; this would be anticipating the future. But the rest of the portrait was approved: the supporting vote was unanimous. Or almost, for one abstained from voting: the Turtle who decidedly could no longer follow …

"But, God, where is he now?" asked a small voice somewhat in panic.

They looked around a bit and the Gazelle was the one who finally replied:

"I just noticed him this moment, walking on the edge of the water, probing the beach, looking for God knows what …"

The Lion led the procession as it filed out two by two. In fact, the Creator was modeling clay.

"This is not much of a success this time," pondered the King of animals but, conscious of his role, he tried not to let anything show.

God nevertheless guessed a little, unless he simply wanted to justify his hands being covered with clay:

"This will be my masterpiece, that is why I put my hand to it personally. All the rest was simply décor."

He thought it over and, not to hurt the feelings of anyone, added: "Or rather the picture frame."

The Lion did not listen, for he was entirely absorbed in the preparation of his flattering speech. First, he apologized for disturbing everyone, presented the creatures' common project, and explained that one animal was going to perform the very first act of piety in everyone's name. This animal would express their common fervor and thus serve as a model throughout the ages. While saying this, the Lion, carried away by his own enthusiasm, made a wide circular gesture that, unknown to him, included the yet shapeless Adam. This first prayer would be used as an example for him too. God frowned, finding that the King's jurisdiction was going a little too far, but he rectified nothing, saying to himself that a lesson is always helpful. There was silence.

What happened next? Was it timidity? Did the Finch want to play down his effects? Did he wait for an absolutely complete silence to make the color of his emotions burst out all the more?

The fact remains that, after a moment when nothing was happening, God, as if he had heard something, suddenly turned to a tree standing nearby and cried out:

"This is exactly the prayer I was hoping for! What a pleasant surprise!"

They were all astonished. They turned around but they saw only a turtledove. Strangled with confusion, the latter was finally able to articulate:

"Me …? But I said nothing. I swear I didn't. I don't even know how to sing. My plumage is dull. And … you, my God, I ask to forgive me if, because of the effects of emotions, I was unable to hold back an 'ouh-ouh' when I saw you."

"You don't know how to make speeches, but you know how to love," the Creator tenderly pointed out. "And that is a language that charms me. What a spokesperson you are for prayer! My friends, your choice delights me. Yes, let the dove teach you how to pray: she is the symbol of love. Someday, I will send my Holy Spirit to teach Humans how to pray. For they will never know how to do so in the correct way. I was wondering what shape I should use to represent him but, thanks to you, I have found one: he will be represented in the form of a dove."

Introduction

Praying is . . .

"Unless there is love, God cannot be found."[1]
Jacques Guillet

Praying is allowing ourselves to be loved. It is to love in return. The two aspects of the same initiative. Here I intend to deal with prayer especially from the second point of view, not that it is the most important one but, alas, we cannot speak about everything at the same time.

To pray, therefore, is to love. Rest assured: the expression is not mine. It threads its way through the whole Christian tradition before it finds its perfect form under Teresa of Avila's pen: "The soul's profit consists not in thinking much but in loving much."[2] Charles de Foucauld brings it back to our attention: "The more we love, the better we pray."[3]

Briefly, it is a love adventure. And, as such, it consists in remaining gently in his company, in conversing without spelling things out, in snuggling in his arms, in burying our face in his open hands, in letting ourselves be taught and cradled by him. It is confiding in him perhaps, but surely listening to him. Or simply, as in any love, to be there, with the beloved, forgetting everything else: "You alone matter."

But here, we are already immersed in the great contemplation. Let us rather start at the beginning.

Prayer is not "thinking much," we are told. Therefore, it is not so much reflecting on God, on his Providence, on his mercy or on some other attribute. Could we imagine a couple of lovers and one suddenly telling the other, "Wait a minute, what you are confiding to me now is so brilliant that I must make note of it." So much the better if some consideration about the Lord sustains our vigilance, but praying does not imply first our reasoning.

If it is love, it is not "speaking much." To be sure, every lover talks. There are even timid ones whom love makes voluble. Because of their limitations, words very soon become obstacles. And we may catch one saying to the other, "Be quiet for a bit, you haven't yet learned simply to be with me?" This is something that the Lord must tell us at times …

Neither is it a matter of concentration. Especially not "concentrating on ourselves"… I am not the one at the center. On the contrary, the other is. Love is a start of astonishment before the beloved. A capacity to wonder. So is prayer, at least in its beginnings: "Surely the Lord is in this place and I did not know it!" (*Gen* 28:16). Of course, there is internalization. And we must plunge into ourselves to find God who dwells in our most intimate being. But what a difference between a tension or an effort to forget everything except ourselves, and a sweet fascination for this Other who dwells within me. Who makes me forget everything outside myself and that is not he.

Basically, prayer is much simpler than this. I am convinced that we know how to pray spontaneously just as we know how to love spontaneously. One moment of profound distress, of wonder or of great joy is enough to make us send a cry to God. So one unforeseen encounter is enough to make us fall head over heels in love … without having learned anything about it beforehand, neither how to pray nor how to love.

Still, in prayer as in love, the most difficult thing is to hold fast. Remaining faithful. Persevering. This is where both become a true labor. When the hum of habit becomes a threat or the sighs of effort become intrusive, then we have to resort to some technique, to some method or procedure to enable us to overcome these obstacles. We have to beg for advice from someone who knows from his own experience. Otherwise, we risk losing both; they may become a withering labor. Starting again persistently every morning. Keeping the oxygen supply going. Briefly, we have to prevent the sacred little flame, which kindled everything in the beginning and for which we long, from going out.

"Still, there was so much warmth in the beginning," the bashful lover will say to himself. "How is it that I no longer feel anything of that?"

"It seemed to me that God was so near at the beginning," the pray-er will also say while he is checking his watch for the third time in five minutes. "How is it that God seems so distant now?"

Normal situations for the one as for the other, provided they do not last too long, since we are on the edge of an abyss. How can we be on our honeymoon again? Usually this is not possible. But neither is an unending desert something to wish for. Ah! If the lover had been able to preserve some of his original affection, had used ingenuity and creativity to do so, throughout the days that wear away and tarnish this love. Had kept a little of this tenderness. Of this attention that keeps the other endeared … And if the pray-er could have done the same with his Father of all goodness, whom he met one day with enthusiasm and who now has become his distant Lord, lost from sight in his routine: if he could have kept some of the tenderness and affection.

A love relationship cannot hold out without affection being received and given.

For prayer is precisely a *love relationship* ...

That is why praying is …

Notes

[1] Jacques Guillet, *Parole de Dieu, paroles d'Église* (Paris: Droguet-Ardant, 1980), p. 52.

[2] *The Complete Works of Saint Teresa of Jesus*, trans. and ed. by E. Allison Peers, 3 vols. (London: Sheed & Ward, 1946), *Book of the Foundations*, vol. 3, chap. 5, p. 20. The same expression is used in *Interior Castle*, Fourth Mansion, vol. 2, chap. 1, p. 233.

[3] Charles de Foucauld, *Écrits spirituels*, 13th ed. (Paris: J. de Girord, 1957), p. 162.

1

... awakening the depths of one's heart

"Come back to your heart.
Perhaps you have already come up,
entered into your heart
and learned to settle there.
Do not let that be enough for you;
learn to remain there."[1]
Anonymous Cistercian,
end of the twelfth century

If you are of a certain age, you probably remember the place where you were when you learned of President Kennedy's assassination on 22 November 1963.

Martin Luther King's widow, Coretta Scott King, describes this moment in her memoirs.[2] Her husband was in the house, attending to some things, the television set was on in the background. She was on the telephone. Suddenly, a special news bulletin announced the tragedy. They spent a long time, seated, watching over and over again the famous pictures that were being constantly projected on the screen. She adds that Martin was very quiet during all this time and finally let it be understood that the same thing would happen to him, that society was sick.

> I was not able to say anything. I had no word to comfort my husband. I could not say, "It won't happen to you." I felt he was right. It was a painfully agonizing silence. I moved closer to him and gripped his hand in mine.[3]

A parable for prayer. Or rather a perfect icon of what it should be.

A moment of such intensity "that there were no words" to express what was being experienced. Nonetheless, a total communion. A similar dagger driven right into the heart, that stops short the breath, that cuts his speech, makes the hand grope around, shaking, in search of another hand. A total communion, indeed, but beyond words. A difficult dive into one's innermost self. There where we are in perfect agreement with the pain that drowns the heart of the other, as our own. We have grasped the other completely. We have expressed everything of ourselves. Still, we said nothing to each other: we could no longer say anything to each other.

This should be our prayer for Good Friday, when we are struck squarely by a nameless distress, when mourning strikes those close to us, when the absurd nature of our human condition overwhelms us and we do not know how to react, so we sit before the Lord. This is one of the greatest prayers that can be.

The huge misery of the poor: entire continents of it … One human being out of two has never heard about the Gospel … The division of the Churches … Terrorism, fierce violence or racism … Going before God and simply sitting there because this is too heavy to bear alone. Hiding oneself in the half-light behind one of the large pillars of the church, to be alone with him. Burying ourselves a little in our cloak as we sink down within ourselves. Being unable to express our pain because of the lump in our throats. And especially, because deep down, we sense that it is beyond expression.

Many believers have never known such intensity in their prayer. Have never experienced with the Lord such a communion in distress (or in joy, as we shall see, or in gratitude) which made of this moment of fervor one that they have never forgotten.

"Peak-Experiences"

"Six years ago, I went on a holiday in the Rockies with my husband."

The eyes of the lady with whom I had been speaking for a few minutes suddenly lit up. I would swear that there were tears if her smile had not told me otherwise. Still, I am certain there was some water in her eyes: an old emotion washed over her face.

"The first morning of our arrival in Banff National Park, I rose early; I was not yet used to the time lag. A thick fog covered all the landscape. Suddenly, the fog rose … and I saw the mountains. I think that for a moment my heart stopped beating. So much grandeur! It was indescribable. It all rose up to the sky: the green of the trees below, the grayness of the rocks on a higher level, steep rocky slopes, breath-taking cliffs, then the whiteness of the snow, such a pure whiteness … finally the blue sky that outlined everything in peaks … How can I tell you this? …"

It seemed that even the wide gestures she used to support her description could not express everything. Then, lowering her eyes with some embarrassment:

"I was told later that I had spent more than two and a half hours, motionless, doing nothing. Looking. Filling my being with these mountains. Nothing else mattered any more, nothing else existed, that was all … only this immensity. It was so gigantic and I felt so small!"

Prayer … Experiencing this vast majesty of God and one's own smallness … Being crushed by it, and astounded at the same time. Astounded especially. Seeing only him, feeling that he exists, that *he alone* exists, and that we are there, so small, *before him*.

Feeling one's breath being taken away. Being unable to say anything. Being distracted by nothing. Feeling projected out of oneself, dazzled by the Other. And at the same time intensely immersed down to our deepest parts, there where something of the other is experienced.

English-speaking people use the expression "*peak-experience*" to describe what this woman lived.

These "peak-experiences" are varied to an infinite degree and exist at all levels of the scale of human existence. It may be on the occasion of an unforeseen bereavement as much as at the moment when we bend over the first cluster of golden yellow crocuses that have just opened out on the brand new spring lawn. It may be at the unveiling of a work of art: a painting by Monet, an allegro by Mozart that we are hearing for the first time, a retort in the theater or a clip from a movie.

It may also be an event of a more religious nature. An elderly priest told me of his first dazzling spiritual moment. This was in the midst of the singing crowd during a grandiose liturgical celebration at the close of a pilgrimage he had made with his parents as a small child. "Hip high," he noted with a laugh. He still remembered it to the extent that should he go back to the site, he could point out precisely the pew where this had happened. Likewise for this young mother for whom the great discovery of God occurred during her childbirth. She sensed with her whole being what the words "God who gives life" mean. As varied as they may be, these "peak-experiences" have certain common characteristics.

The first, as we have already noted, is that *time flies.* One has to spend two and a half hours on one's feet gazing, motionless, without a change of scene … And not be bored either … On the contrary, this time will always be too short, and, if we must leave, we will feel frustration, a wrenching away.

The second one is that we are not *attracted by anything else*, even if we are all but directly entreated.

"Standing before these huge cliffs, it was as if I had forgotten everything: the trip, home, children, work, even my husband and even breakfast … This all happened by itself. I felt so good deep down in myself that everything else seemed to have disappeared."

Nothing else exists any more or, in any case, nothing else can make any claims on us. If I compare this with prayer, I could say that there are no "distractions," but let us not anticipate too much. Let us be content to note that when we are immersed in a peak-experience, we well know that the world keeps on turning, that our companions are there, and that a thousand cares await us, but it is as if nothing is worth being concerned about.

The third characteristic of these peak-experiences is that they are extremely *fulfilling*.

"That happened many years ago but I remember it as if it were yesterday. And since then we, my husband and I, have come back every year. We always say that we should really go somewhere else one of these days, but I do not dare take the risk. It is so beautiful out there."

"But your husband?"

"He likes to sun himself on a lounge chair."

"He must find the sun warmer in Florida …"

"Yes, but he tells me that 'my' mountains do me so much good that he no longer knows me when I get back home. So …"

We may apply this characteristic especially to the experiences that have a positive effect (artistic discoveries, esthetic wonderment, feelings of sympathy, etc.). However, I do not totally exclude those that are more trying and which, even if we are aware of this only years later, bring us a wealth of humanization.

Still another particular trait is that they are relatively *rare*. We do not have two or three of them every day. Besides, this would be emotionally unbearable, we would explode: "Let me breathe …" In any case, we are unable to produce them at will.

"And it is the same every time?"

"It has never been like the first time. That is not possible, it was too much. There is always something similar to it, but like the first time, no."

We can go back as much as we like to the same scene, put ourselves again in the same setting, but the magic moment will not be there for all that.

The "Peak-Prayer"

My apologies. I have just promised in the introduction not to start with prayer that is too highly contemplative, and here we are right smack into it. Too late to go back …

The fact is that prayer belongs to the same order of things. Or rather that certain moments of prayer, when the latter becomes particularly intense, are like these peak-experiences. Something most exceptional I admit. This happens once or twice in a whole lifetime. At the most, four or five if you are privileged. I would call that a "peak-prayer."

I remember having experienced such a moment. I must have been seven or eight years old. The breeze of a brand new spring day had driven me, from the height of my little legs, a little farther than usual, to a small grove a few hundred meters away from the house. As I entered it, I was suddenly surrounded with a fabulous pale green carpet covered with a constellation of little blue, yellow and white flowers. I remained frozen on the spot. There were some as far as the eye could see. An abundance of them, each being a masterpiece in itself. I could never have imagined that there could be so many in the whole world. And they were all there, within reach.

How amazing is the Creator! We cannot see him, and if nature is only his cloak, how splendid he must be! If he can make so many flowers without anyone asking him to and without anyone even knowing he is doing so, what would he not do for me just for the asking?

I am putting into words in this way, *a posteriori*, what I felt in the deepest recess of my little heart as a little child, which had suddenly become too big for my chest. But I remember very clearly that I said nothing about it. In any case words would have failed me if I had tried. I did not speak of God who, all of a sudden, was everywhere. Perhaps I cried. In wonder.

I have no memory of the first time I went to the parish church. I do not remember my first communion either. I have forgotten almost everything of my first catechism. But I can still describe, as if it were yesterday, this precise moment when, on the edge of the forest, God became the big, the vast *Someone*. Someone active and attentive to the least little thing, even a minute flower lost in the sea of its fellow-flowers.

Have no fear! You have no reason to be jealous: that experience never occurred again. Therefore, I am not an exceptional being upon whom the graces of heaven have come down in showers.

Forty years later, I see this event as a basic phase of my spiritual journey: one of the foundations of my monastic life. This carpet of humble spring flowers still teaches me how to pray …

Not that I can experience it again: by definition it remains unique. Nor even that I can experience something similar every time I set about to pray: this would be too beautiful. But it points out from afar, *from a very great distance*, a direction for me to take. Since that moment and for all my life, I have a model, although beyond reach, towards which I must aspire. I try to reach it. That is all God asks of me.

Perhaps you have a similar page in the holy history of your life. Do you know how to draw inspiration from it?

The Depths of the Heart

Let us point out a final characteristic of the peak-experiences: they drive us down into *the depths of our heart*.[4]

Speaking about the depths of this heart is not easy. We have an *interior space* in ourselves that I would describe as "psychosomatic" where our deep emotions take us. Not the more or less exalting flutters that affect us at every turn, but this emotional impulse that drives us into the deepest part of ourselves and that puts us on the lookout for everything that might draw us to the surface. It is as if our whole being were monopolized by this emotion, as if all the "fluid" of our consciousness were focused on it in this inner space where this emotion overwhelms us.

Some mystics have spoken of it as of an "abyss," an "interior ocean" in which we immerse ourselves, a "well" the breathtaking depths of which constantly draw us down. The predominant psychological impression is that we "are going down" there. We "sink" in there, we "lose" ourselves there like a sponge thrown into the sea, they say. I will come back to this language of immersion to deal with our subject.

We could have spoken of this in a different way. When love impulses, the burning of the heart, predominate, we feel "aspired" upwards. Other spiritual masters have looked for their images in the sense of height. They speak of the "summit of the spirit" or of the "fine peak" of the soul. In order to avoid confusion, I will not use this vocabulary: we simply remember that it is possible.

But all that does not do much to clarify things. Let us go back to experience. Coretta King, at the moment related above, was immersed in the depths of her heart. The lady in love with the Rockies, like the tiny child that I was, and including the aesthete who is reached by a work of art and the film enthusiast by a movie, all of us were, at the moment recalled, set in the profound depths of our heart.

And you are there when you are bereaved, when you are distressed. Do we not say at that moment that our "heart is heavy"? You are there when you are filled with a great joy.

It is the site of your strong feelings: joy, grief, admiration, wonder, fear.

This is the site where you love. It is the place in yourselves that is set in motion, that begins to vibrate when this feeling of being in love fills you.

Finally, it is God's site, the place where God can touch you. The place where, unknown to you, he is always in touch with you. God reaches you from within even when what speaks to you about him comes from without.

Therefore it is also the site for prayer. "Go down into your heart and there, go to God," St. Augustine tells us. Most of the time we pray with the superficial parts of ourselves. The prayer is then restless and unstable. We find difficulty in persisting in it. Time drags. We are always "gone." We have "to recollect ourselves" constantly.

Yet the lady of the Rockies experienced no difficulty in staying on. She did not complain about having distractions. Could she not teach us something about prayer?

Could not our own experiences teach us something? For example, *how to find the way to the depths of our hearts*?

Note that I do not claim that prayer is identified with a strong emotion. Absolutely not. Nor even that there is a cause and effect link between the two. On the contrary, the deeper the prayer, the more sober it becomes, as we will have the opportunity of demonstrating. My intention is simply to show that both *spring from the same depth.*

Have you ever noticed that in certain extreme situations *something is praying on within you*? Almost unknown to you. You move imperceptibly from the overwhelming feeling to prayer even if you have little faith, even none at all. This is because you have come down to the precise place within yourself where emotions and prayer take their flight. Their birthplaces are identical.

When you are spellbound before a landscape, it is almost natural for you to break out in thanksgiving for the Creator. The amazement makes you go down to the hollow depths of your being, and that is where, at the center, you begin to pray almost spontaneously. Or rather, it is the center that begins to pray. The heart is praying …

Another example. When you are under the shock of a trial, petition springs up almost in spite of yourself. Pain has taken you totally to the site of the heart. That is where prayer arises. You slip from a wounded love (from the cause that distresses you) to a petitioning love (in prayer). Your love changes its emphasis somewhat, but it is the same love that rises from one sole organ. *The site where we love is always the same.* This is the one I suggest that you try to find. Prayer goes on by itself there. Or almost.

The Organ of Prayer

Still I must admit that I have been doing some bluffing. If you have followed me closely until now, you are about to believe that contemplative prayer comes with an avalanche of strong emotions. It is time now to straighten out your impression.

Prayer is a peak-experience, indeed, but of a very special type. Let me illustrate this with a few cases that are like it.

- You are standing at the window of your living room and you keep on admiring the first snowfall coming down in large snowflakes, like cotton batten, gradually transforming the ground into a sea of cotton.
- You are alone in the house in the evening, seated comfortably doing nothing. Over the loudspeakers you hear a selection of Gregorian music that carries you away in its pattern that is serene, grave and majestically intertwined all at the same time.
- You are away from everything, on the shore of a lake decked in its October colors. The setting sun suddenly shoots a shaft of light between the hills and transforms the landscape into an interplay of burning flames.

In each of these three cases, you experience something very special which, even in our everyday language, will be expressed in terms of "contemplation": "I was in contemplation before …"

And now, if I ask you what you felt at that moment, you will answer me:

"Nothing. Nothing except a great inner peace. A great calm and a great serenity."

And yet, you are nonetheless in the depths of your heart. If I used an image, I would say that there are many doors leading into the heart. There is the main door at the front. This is for important visitors: people entering it cause a great stir. A guest coming through this door alerts the whole house: effusions and great emotion. But, a little further back, there is the side door. We go through this one more discreetly without ringing the doorbell. Regular inmates of the house use it, people whom, with time, we no longer notice.

Some events come in through the main door. Others, like the three I have just listed, through the side door. For the lady of the Rockies, the mountains came in the first time through the main door, thus creating a whole unforeseen excitement. Then, gradually more often, through the side door, creating only a strong impression of inner calm.

God also, at times, comes in through the main door. He manifests himself to our sensibility that reacts in praise and exultation. Then as he becomes an inmate of the household, as we become familiar with his visits, emotions, as it were, become suspended. His advent is then a moment when "there is no longer anything, unless a feeling of peace."

Only as we become accustomed to this state do we recognize him more and more easily … and speak less and less about the experience. Does not our growing familiarity with his presence in the center of our being free us from our strong emotions and take us to another form of relationship, less sensitive and more internalized?

We are always in the depths of the heart, this spiritual organ where the most secret encounters between God and us occur. But it is not a matter of "winding ourselves up to develop an inner warmth." Nor to experience tempestuous emotions: sighing, crying. Still less to be carried away by an inner hurricane, burning and enkindling the whole being. It is rather a matter of living in a state of appeasement and serenity, of silent recollection and peace as St. John of the Cross teaches us:

> And this peace [God's], being spiritual and delicate, performs a work which is quiet and delicate, solitary, productive of peace and satisfaction [...] This is the peace which, says David, God speaks in the soul.[5]

Henceforth, the attraction we feel for his presence in us is what tells us of his coming: an attraction that does not arise only from our emotions. The presence of the Lord is not always obvious to the senses, but it always imposes itself by a I-know-not-what in our innermost selves, something which defies definitions and is almost indescribable. But so real! What is experienced in the depths of one's heart from now on is summed up in a *loving attention* that is the contemplative attitude *par excellence*.

Before the sight of falling snow or of the setting sun, you spontaneously immersed yourself deep into your inner being, while, on the contrary, in the case of contemplative prayer you must learn to do it. If you do not learn to place prayer in your own inner depths, you will ultimately believe that it amounts to waging a warfare against your distractions, a warfare in which, besides, you will always be the loser ...

> I remember you writing to me that you would develop a headache whenever you tried to sustain your attention. This is what happens when you work only with your head; but if you go down into your heart, you will no longer have any difficulty. Your head will become empty and your thoughts will run dry. They are always in the head, chasing one another, and you cannot manage to control them. But if you go down into your heart, and if you are able to stay there,

> then every time thoughts will invade your head, you will only have to go down into your heart and the thoughts will fly away. You will find yourself in a haven of comfort and security. Do not be slothful, go down there. Life is found in the heart, and that is where you must live.[6]

Having confessed my bluff, I hope things are clearer now. Try to recall a short moment when you really felt you were in the presence of God. The memory of a small puff of intense prayer lasting fifteen or thirty seconds will be enough. Not necessarily a peak-prayer: a short instant when there was no longer anyone but him alone, and when *you felt good with him*. This happens to anyone praying and is nothing exceptional.

Try to recall as well as you can the experience of that precise moment, and then ask yourself the following questions:

• *Where was I within myself?* What was going on in me? Where was this taking place? What part of my being was in a vibrant state? Where was I aware of being concentrated? Think of this "heavy heart," but do so soberly.[7]

• *What did I do to get there*? What psychic road did I take?

• And finally, how could I go back there again the next time I pray?

Difficult? Do not worry, I will accompany you in the next pages. My personal experience teaches me that all that is at stake in prayer is found here.

First be aware that this interior space where God is waiting for us exists. When prayer carries us away, when words fail us or when we are bathing in the peace of God's presence, we are inevitably there. But still we must become conscious of this place. Otherwise, we will be groping every time we set about praying. But once this is done, whenever we wish to pray, we will simply have to go back to this place in ourselves. Prayer will come spontaneously.

This does not mean that, in my case, I do this every time … but that is another story!

Praying Is As Simple As Loving

We pray very naturally. However, explaining prayer is very difficult.

For example, a couple of people in love have a tête-à-tête candlelight dinner. A few roses, some background music, subdued lighting and the aroma of breaded scallops are enough to create the atmosphere.

Should not every one of our encounters with God tend towards the cordial intimacy we find in lovers? It is impossible to attain this. Let us, nonetheless, use them as models, little does it matter if we rarely succeed. After all, neither are all our meals candlelight dinners …

Let us listen to them. They tell each other how happy they are to be together. The quiet joy they have in seeing each other again. In no way are they discussing the big news of the day; far from them the debate over the major problems of society. They set their hearts on the same wavelength by sharing their mutual feelings. A simple cordial sharing.

Should not our prayer adopt the same path? Rather than chatting about everything and nothing, let us confide to him what moves us, concerns and rejoices us. We will have a better chance of being on the road to the heart.[8]

But now they are hardly talking any more. We will have to move closer to hear them better. Indeed. There is still a word now and then. Murmured rather than said. Almost read on the lips. Interrupted by long periods of silence. But silences loaded with an overflow of feelings, as it were.

Could not our prayer be condensed in a few words, in a compliment, in a simple call? Even in one single word, the whole value of which would reside in its being set in the jewel case of long periods of silence preceding and following it and giving it its luster?[9]

One would swear now that all they are doing is gazing at each other. Yet, they do not seem to be bored. Nor have anything more to say. Their lips are silent except to smile, and their eyes bask in each other's gaze.

Would we be able to find happiness in looking at him, and in letting ourselves be looked at by him? Would we be able to let his loving gaze be wrapped around us and read his response to our distresses in his eyes watching over us?[10]

But they are not only gazing at each other. Now, their fingers are seeking those of the other, are touching each other, are interlacing. All is done gently and delicately, the hands of both of them are joined, caressed and borne to the other's lips.

Would we be able to place our hands in his, our dried and empty hands, so that he may welcome and warm them up, our callous and idle hands, so that he may do what he wishes with them, remodeling them in his own way?[11]

Let us note finally that nothing seems to distract them from each other. To the extent that they do not even hear the television in the neighboring apartment, the noise of which would make them cross in any other circumstance.

And all these concerns they thought to be so absorbing, these issues about the budget, the files to prepare, errands to run, no longer even touch their minds. All the more reason not to preoccupy their hearts. They are totally centered on the other and the other alone is in their hearts.

The True Challenge in Prayer

Oh! The beautiful definition of prayer here: "Their heart is totally centered on the Other and the Other alone is in their hearts." I do not claim to say that we achieve this often. This happens on extremely rare occasions, as I know from experience. And still, I really like this expression. It indicates once more an ideal, what there is at the end of the road. It is useful to know where the way to prayer leads us if we really wish to find it. Thus we will be *drawn* in the right direction as by a magnet.[12]

Defining prayer in this way allows us to unmask all the false excuses we make up to justify our mediocrity: lack of time, the weight of our responsibilities, the noisy atmosphere … and that is not all.

Whereas new lovers always manage to find the means to meet, there is a central point set aside for this rendez-vous, however brief it may be. They may be right in the middle of their examination session, yet their whole day will be planned in relation to those few minutes spent together.

We may conclude that the true reason preventing us from meeting Christ is not really a lack of time. "We always find time to do what we like," as the saying goes.

The young girl expecting a telephone call from her friend who is away? The worst racket will not prevent her from hearing it ring and running to answer it even if this happens during the grand New Year's family *party* while three little nieces are yelling beside her. She will hear it. She will even be the only one to hear it. You would think that the heart is the one who hears …

Are we still able to hear the call of the Lord who loves us in the midst of the noise we entertain even within ourselves? "We hear what we wish to hear," again as the saying goes. "No one is harder of hearing that the one who refuses to hear." Do we really want to hear?

And the young man at a party … All the guests are wearing black and white, only "she" is dressed in colors. Have you ever been to a cocktail party and know that your "flame" (especially if it has not yet been made known) is some ten feet away from you? You are no longer listening to those discussing with you, you have ears only for what is being said over there … Again the heart is the one listening, yes, indeed …

When we say that we are totally taken up by our many tasks, would it not be rather that the heart is not exactly where the Gospel expects it to be? "Where your treasure is, there your heart will be also" (*Mt* 6:21).

We lay the blame on lack of time and I know not what else. Basically, if something is preventing us from praying, would it not be because we are not sufficiently in love?

I would like very much to have this kind of love, but I admit I do not have it. I would like to make this kind of prayer, but I do not do it either. It depends … At least, when I face the problem in this way, I know where things are going wrong.

Lovers are not the only ones that stimulate me. There is also the scientist about to bring an experiment to a successful conclusion. The woman student preparing for an important examination. The lawyer building up a case.

When I am with my brothers and sisters, I sometimes set aside what I am doing to be with them. Especially if I have not seen that person for a long time: I find time … Why not for the Lord? When I worry about someone close to me who is in the hospital, I find myself thinking of him constantly. Why so much neglect when it is a matter of thinking of God? We could multiply examples of this kind.

Every comparison falls short and these like the others. They present to us a prayer that touches the sublime. But I say to myself that if I am satisfied with being where I am, I will never improve, and it is only by looking far ahead that I will ultimately get there.

Notes

[1] Attributed to St. Bernard, *De Domo interiori seu de Conscientia.*

[2] Coretta Scott King, *My Life with Martin Luther King, Jr.* (New York: Holt, Rinehart and Winston, 1969).

[3] *Ibid.*, p. 244.

[4] I am deliberately not using the word "heart" all by itself because its modern connotations are too close to "sensibility," but I am using "depths of the heart" to be nearer to the biblical sense of the word.
"In our present manner of speaking, 'heart' evokes only the emotional life. In [the Bible], the heart is perceived as the 'interior life' of man in a much broader sense. Besides feelings, the heart also holds memories and ideas, projects and decisions. [...] It is the center of being, the place where man holds a dialogue with himself, assumes his responsibilities, opens or closes himself to God." X.-L. Dufour, ed., *Vocabulaire de théologie biblique* (Paris: Cerf, 1977), Article "cœur," p. 175.

[5] *The Complete Works of St. John of the Cross*, trans. and ed. by E. Allison Peers, 3 vols. (Westminster, Maryland: The Newman Press, 1953), *Dark Night of the Soul*, vol. 1, pp. 354-355.

[6] Theophane the Recluse, quoted in Igumen Chariton of Valaam, *L'art de la prière* (Bellefontaine Abbey, 1976), p. 253.

[7] We can say that in most people this takes place at the base of the sternum. Besides, it is there, at the level of the stomach, that religions of the Far East place the center of being, and teach their people who meditate to focus their inner gaze. But this is not absolute; in some people, this may be

a little higher, in the upper part of the chest, even under the skin of the face. While we experience strong emotions, we will have the impression that this spot is warming up. Nonetheless, do not be too persistent in determining this "physical" location, since it is above all a "psychic" place. But there remains the fact that most are able to locate it quite accurately in their body.

[8] We will deal with this at greater length in the next chapter.

[9] This topic will be discussed in chapter three.

[10] We will expand on this idea in chapter four.

[11] The proper gestures to be used in prayer will be considered in chapters five and six.

[12] By a play on two senses of the word "drawn": drawn as by a magnet and drawn by affection.

2

... conversing with him

"I know there are many people
who practice vocal prayer ...
and are raised by God
to the higher kind of contemplation
without having
any hand in this themselves
or even knowing
how it has happened."[1]
St. Teresa of Avila

I am ready to wager that the first time you caught yourself praying to God, you were *speaking* to him. And I run no risk of losing my wager since this was so obvious.

As we will have the opportunity of seeing, prayer does not amount to "speaking to God." Even if every prayer, and especially the one beginning to emerge, takes the form of a statement addressed to him. Speaking to him with familiar terms as in so many examples offered to us by the Bible.

It is well and truly speaking as a friend speaks to his friend or a servant to his master. Now we ask for a grace, then we accuse ourselves of something not properly done, at yet another time we confide our affairs and ask for advice thereon.[2]

So, like two friends. Prayer must be made with ease, simplicity, respectful familiarity and it must be natural, spontaneous and straightforward as in a conversation between people who are on familiar terms. All of them feel that they are in a happy complicity.

Or again like two lovers. Love "exists without words" but it is better when it is expressed. Two individuals in love, each knowing that he or she is loved by the other, never grow weary telling each other so. They are amazed at what is happening to them; they say so to each other again and again in every possible way; they even invent a language understood by them alone.

Their love has to be expressed in words. It may be silent but never speechless. It will always need to be declared, and this will be done by way of confidences.

The content of what they say is not what is important, it is the fact of telling each other about it. Besides, if we managed to catch them sitting on a bench in the park and declaring their love, and we recorded everything they said, we would find nothing more stupid. They are learning nothing new from each other. It is by constantly restating their love that they make it exist. Years later, one might say to the other, "you never told me that you loved me." It is not that proofs are lacking, it is that love is no longer declared, the declaration being an essential part of it.

We understand Charles de Foucauld's distress when he wrote in his diary at the end of his life, "I tell him so often that I love him and he never tells me he does."

Confide in Him

If I love you or if I simply trust you, I will confide my intimate self to you. But I will do so only inasmuch as I love you. There are no confidences without love and there is no love without confidences. I could even measure my degree of intimacy with So-and-so among my companions by assessing the nature and the quantity of my confidences to him. Believe me, this is an excellent barometer.

Revelation is God revealing what he is to man. This reaches you through preaching or through the meditated reading of Scripture. The latter is called *lectio divina* and is not only "spiritual reading," but is truly "divine reading," or better yet, "reading God."

In this *lectio*, God is confiding to you what he is, the vibrations of his heart, the secrets of his mystery.

Prayer is confiding in him in return. It is not merely the recitation of formulas, however beautiful they may be, but the expression of what you are, of what dwells in you at this moment, of your anxieties, of your desires and joys. Small things most of the time, sometimes great ones.

Not to teach him anything, but so that the relationship may continue to exist. Nor to inform him of some event concerning you that perhaps, totally by chance, he might not have seen, but so that your love for him might pass through the words you address to him. Very simply.

Like a couple, finding each other again in the evening for supper, each of them having had a full day, and telling each other what went on in the office or elsewhere. Things that happen in the office are seldom extraordinary. Most of the time, the day was just the same as the previous one, of a distressing banality. And yet there is this need to share these events, the need for the one to express them and for the other to listen.

Nothing unusual has happened, but what is important is that the loved one confide in the other, and it is by talking about the day that he tells the other – without using many words – that he loves that person and places his trust in him or her. Since he agrees to confide himself in the other, he relates even the most trivial details.

If, before you fall asleep in the evening, you tell the Lord about your day, your goal is not to teach him anything. He knows who you are, what is going on inside you, what happened to you during the day that you are now handing over into his hands. But by telling him all that, you are saying to him – without saying so in precise words – that you are placing your trust in him, that he has a place in your life. And that you love him.

You Are Expressing More Than What Your Words Are Saying

Linguistics teaches us that when we are speaking to another person, we are always expressing something fundamental to that person, something that is not in the words we are using.[3]

Let us consider the simplest example possible: on the street across from the shopping center, I meet a neighbor who lives on the same floor as I do. We have no particular ties, but we know each other at least by sight. I greet him, "Good morning, the weather is nice today."

If this neighbor is not totally stupid, he has also probably noticed that the sun is shining. And since I am not too stupid either, I presume he knows that as well as I do. Still I tell him, "The weather is nice." But when I am saying that, my purpose is not so much to give him some meteorological information about the weather which, by chance, he might not have noticed, but to tell him *something else*. For example, "I recognize you and you are not completely indifferent to me. We are not great friends, but neither are we total strangers. If you ever need me, let me know, do not hesitate …"

Note that while not all is said, it is nonetheless expressed … and understood by both of us. If, when I saw him coming, I had turned away from him to the shop window, the neighbor would have known where he stood with me. He would have felt hurt and rightly so. Not that he would have missed some interesting information about the weather, but he would have understood that I was cutting off our good neighbor *relationship*. *Saying nothing* is also a way of making ourselves understood. A message is passed on in our refusal to speak and people know very well how to interpret it even if nothing is said.

I leave you now to imagine all that is implied in the simple fact of agreeing to say a brief word to the Lord, even before taking the content of what you will say into account. Be it only to say to him, "Good morning, Lord." The whole difference is between telling him, "Good morning, the weather is nice today," and saying nothing at all to him, turning away, when we feel he is approaching us.

Let us consider a second example. A boy, more familiar with the urban environment than with other things, scares a frog out of its hiding while taking a walk with his father in the forest. He tries to catch it, but as we may expect, it escapes him by leaping into the nearby stream. Immediately, he rushes to his father and tells him, gasping for breath and with a profusion of gestures, how big the frog was and how it jumped far away from him when he tried to grasp it in his hand.

His father, who has seen more than one frog in his days, is learning nothing new from his son's breathless speech. He has known for a long time that a frog does not let itself be trapped so easily and that, if we try to catch it, it jumps out of reach. Still, he lets his child tell him the whole story as if he were learning everything about it at the same time as his son. And the child tells him twice over rather than once. And he listens and asks questions, with a broad smile.

Beyond what is being *said*, which is, after all, only about a poor little frog, are they not in the process of *experiencing* a *father-son* relationship? And if the father finds so much delight in the repetitive chatter of his child, is it not because something is being expressed in this talk which, while not being said in the words used, nevertheless is using these words to express itself?

If you have the impression sometimes that you have nothing to confide to the Lord, or the sensation that what you are telling him is sheer rambling, that this is useless since he already knows everything about you, are you not forgetting that beyond what you are telling him, you are speaking to him only because you are in a filial relationship with him? That this relationship, impossible to formulate no matter what words are used because it is always beyond us, nonetheless uses your trivial talk to express itself.

Even if you are unaware of this, the Father knows. And he listens to you with a smile of wonder. You may tell him the same thing twice and three times over, he will always listen to you. And for him, this will always be new. Each time will be a discovery for him. No. It will be more than that. A wonder: his child is speaking to him.

And here is a last example. You surely must have experienced something similar to this. One of your friends was in a car accident a few days ago: a rollover and everything that comes with it, strong emotions, but no serious injuries, fortunately.

Now this friend comes to see you. Since this is his first visit since the famous accident, you are not supposed to know anything about it yet. But it so happens that you have a mutual friend who has already described to you the whole incident in minute detail. Nevertheless, you play the game, you act as if you knew nothing and you let him tell you the whole story.

Why do you pretend in this way? Out of vulgar deceit? Surely not. No question either of accusing you of hypocrisy since I know very well that, on your part, your attitude is in line with the best of friendships. So is this flattery or double play?

Nothing like that. Instinctively and because of the esteem you have for your friend, you have given him the opportunity, not only of relating these facts again, but also of experiencing once more the avalanche of heartthrobs associated with them. Of reliving them *before* you and *with* you by letting him tell you the details. In some way, you have allowed him to be no longer alone in this adventure, but to have someone with him in the vehicle. Someone dear to him, who is able to listen and sympathize, able to understand and be compassionate. Since you agree to let him tell you about the incident.

Does not the Lord let you tell him your story? Does he not constantly give you the opportunity to experience again your adventures, great and small, before and with him? Finally, could we not say that, as he listens to you, he agrees to be "with you in the vehicle?"

In Matthew's Gospel, Jesus declares that "Your heavenly Father knows that you need all those things" (*Mt* 6:32). And still, a few verses later, in the same gospel, "Ask …" *(Mt* 7:7). Apparently illogical: if he knows, why must we still ask? Unless the Father's wish is precisely to hear us asking. I feel like translating this as follows: "The Father already knows everything that has happened to you … tell him …" Are we ready to do so?

"Ask," Says Jesus

Do we even agree to ask? Speaking of prayer, most of the time the New Testament and the whole Bible mention only the prayer of petition. Yet, our scientific era has taught us that God respects secondary causes. He does not bungle the laws of nature in order to respond to our whims every time we pray to him. Has biblical teaching gone out of style? We consider ourselves to be adult believers for whom the prayer of petition is only a childlike phase of prayer. A phase we are expected to outgrow as soon as possible. Have we possibly forgotten this law of psychology, that "a petition hides another petition?"

What is a child who wants his mother to tie his shoelaces, although with a little effort he could manage this on his own, really asking for if not that his mother give him a little of her attention? Whether she ties his laces or not, he will get a little hug from her. Do not psychologists tell us that "every request is first of all a request for love?"

You pray to God to tie your shoelaces … and here he agrees to be present to you. God *does not always give* but he *gives of himself* every time, which is much more. He cannot do otherwise; this is in his nature.

I knew a child who had been brought up to the rhythm of blows. These blows were the only relationship he had with his parents. At school, he behaved in such a way so as to "earn" some on a regular basis. He was happy only when he was hit, and then he smiled with contentment. To draw blows was the only way he had learned to get attention. By getting one, he could say, "Bravo, I exist."

We are all in need of esteem, gratitude and consideration. To get all that, we use a trick: we go by way of a request for something else. We pretend we need something that, in our opinion, the person asked could well agree to give us. Often without being aware of this, we are, in fact, begging for a small dose of attention. And the latter we hope will be given to us when the requested object is given to us. An object we apparently want first but which, in reality, comes in second place.

A new tenant has arrived in your apartment building. You like her looks and you would like to meet her. You search for means to do this. You use this old trick which has proved its worth: you go and borrow something from her. Here, you ask for a cup of sugar.

Suppose she gave you this cup, then closed the door in your face without saying a word to you. Still, you have what you asked for … It seems to me that your request has been "granted"…

When you beg God for something like this cup of sugar, do you really expect to be given only sugar? If your heavenly Father cannot always give you sugar, on the other hand he always gives "good things to those who ask him" (*Mt* 7:11). Without their being aware of having asked for it or of having received it. But you do not realize that these are the "good things" you were asking for.

I dare to ask for anything from an intimate or a close friend while agreeing beforehand that my request may not always be granted. I even accept this without any difficulty since we know each other. But I could not accept being neither welcomed nor listened to.

God knows our way of operating. He knows we are asking for more, and for something altogether different from what we seem to request. For he knows that what we desire is beyond words, but that we have to use words to express our petition. He knows, so he always grants what we *desire* (without our knowing how to ask him), being unable to give what we *are asking for* every time (for lack of knowing how to express what we wish). That is why our petitions must hollow out the utter depths of our heart in order to dig out this desire unknown to ourselves.

Still, concerning the relevance of the prayer of petition, I would go yet further. During the last decades, people in many groups of faithful have loved to say that the act of thanksgiving and praise are forms of prayer superior to petition. They believe these to be more devoid of self-interest and to be given more freely. They believe these to be worthier of us and of God's majesty.

I admit that I thought this way for a long time. But the more I reflect on this, the less I agree with it. And that is so precisely because of the nature of our God: he is a person. And also because of our bond with him: an interpersonal relationship. We may praise Cosmic Energy or give thanks to a "god" of this type. But we can address a petition only to a personal God. To a God who listens. Who loves, who responds.

Jesus knew what he was doing when he urged us to ask. He knew that by dint of asking, we would ultimately place our trust in him. This was his goal. Once we trusted him, we would know how to ask. Knowing how to ask is not to harass him to obtain trifles, but ultimately to solicit him to give us what he wants us to desire truly: to possess him. And his love. To become like him forever.

Nothing is absolutely necessary for us except to be loved by God.

> We need you, you alone and no one else [...] All of us need you, even those who are unaware of this need; much more those who are unaware of this than those who know. The hungry man believes he is looking for bread and he yearns for you; the thirsty man imagines he wants water and he thirsts for you; the sick man is under the illusion that he desires to be healthy and his pain is your absence. Those in this world who are seeking the beautiful are unknowingly looking for you, for you are the complete and perfect beauty. Those who in their thoughts pursue the truth are pursuing you who are the only truth worth knowing. And those who

are reaching out for peace are reaching out to you who are the only peace where hearts may be at rest. They are calling for you, unaware that they are calling you.[4]

Have we ever become conscious of that? That what God wants us to ask for is God himself?

"The fool prays to obtain what he desires, the wise man prays to desire what he obtains." A beautiful proverb from the Eastern World. Jesus was not familiar with it, but he would have loved it … "Do not heap up empty phrases as the Gentiles do … your Father knows what you need … good things …"

Be Simple and True

Since the prayer discussed here is a heart-to-heart affair, do not try to be lengthy – or brief – but try to be true. Avoid long prayers that, basically, do not express what you truly feel.

"Lord, I love you more than everything else; take my heart, it is yours totally …"

"Really …"

On some days, the truth will consist in saying, "Lord, I love you," and on others, "Lord, I do not love you."

In the last century, people repeated inflated expressions of this kind: "Lord, I offer myself to you, my whole being, as a sacrifice of atonement and as a living host, in reparation for sacrileges and blasphemies …" and the prayer went on like that … Fortunately, God did not answer our prayer …

Do not say, "Lord, give me the virtue of humility," if, in fact, you do not at all wish to receive it. In this case, say rather, “Lord, I do not really want to be humble, but I know that I need to become so; grant that I may desire to be so.”

You run the risk that God might hear you.

I even consider this last prayer to be one of the most dangerous there is: it ties in with what God wants for us and he will be unable for very long to resist the temptation to afflict us with what we are asking of him. And we would be in a very bad fix … in contrast to the two previous ones which, in spite of their frightening appearance, could have no other effect than to make us burst into laughter. “Do not heap up empty phrases as the Gentiles do; for they think that they will be heard because of their many words …” (*Mt* 6:7).

We must admit that listening to the sublime things we say is enough to make one die of laughter: “Lord, I love you above all things … I firmly believe everything the Holy Church believes and teaches …”

Rather say, “Lord, I believe but help me in my lack of faith.” Or again, “I am blind, make me see. I am deaf, make me hear. I am sick with leprosy, cleanse me of my ills.” This will be closer to the Gospel.

Go up to him and say, “Lord, I am sorry, but you bore me. Lord, I am coming to meet you. But I am warning you right away: I will not stay long. If you do nothing to hold me back, in two minutes I will be gone again. You see, I have just come and I am already beginning to be bored. I told you so. Besides, it seems to me that, all of a sudden, I have heaps of things to do … so make me stay. Keep me for a while. Teach me how to pray.”

Express Your Feelings

Growth in intimacy with God will come by way of the pains you take to expose your emotions, your reactions, your feelings in depth. Do not remain on the surface of things, go down into your own depths and try to expose to him whatever you discover there. The important thing is not the order of words or ideas, but the intensity you put into them. The lips must reach the heart so that each word may be an experienced and living word.

The more intimate we are with someone, the more we confide in him, not only facts, but also our *feelings related to these facts*.

Stable relationships, like marriage, are built on the sharing of intimate feelings. Should one of the partners, because of an emotional blockage of some sort, find it difficult to communicate in this area, he sometimes has to have recourse to some outside help to overcome this difficulty.

Hand over to the Lord not only the events of the day, but also especially what you *feel* about these events: fear, joy, worry and restlessness, weariness or gratitude. Do not say, "Lord, help me, I must hand in a report to my boss tomorrow." Tell him, "Lord, I feel worried and depressed about this business of the report, give me serenity."

"Bring the intellect down into the heart," the startzi[5] of the Eastern Churches tell us. What does this mean? Do *not* worry about your projects, concerns or troubles as such. Keep your intellect busy with what *you are feeling*. In this way, you will go down into your heart. There, tell God everything. Entrust everything to him. Then, *repeat it all*.

Tell him you love him or that you would like to love him. Say this again and again. Remain in your heart. Respect these *short intervals of silence* that come up between your declarations. Let your emotions echo in these short intervals of silence. *Make yourself more and more attentive to them*. Gradually become familiar with them …

We know very little about what Jesus said to his Father when he prayed, but the few samples we have are more than revealing. "Jesus rejoiced in the Holy Spirit […] and said: I thank you, Father …" (*Lk* 10:21). "He began to be grieved and agitated […] he prayed saying, 'My Father, if it is possible …'" (*Mt* 26:37-39). The emotion was intense to a rare degree, we must admit.

In this sense, the psalms are unparalleled masterpieces. It must be noted that the psalmist rarely informs us about the precise circumstances of the distress at the source of his lament. At times, we sense that it is about an illness,[6] or a moral suffering.[7] Elsewhere, he declares that he is crushed by false accusations,[8] or surrounded by enemies.[9] But if you are eager for details, you will have to use your imagination. It is all the same when he breaks into a song of thanksgiving. If he proclaims loudly that God has delivered him, just go and find out from what … here, it seems to be from death,[10] there, it would be rather from those who accuse him, who have been put to flight.[11] Lastly, elsewhere, there is no means of knowing.[12] If we have no details about the circumstances (a fact, let me say in passing, that allows each of us to adopt a text so distant from us in time and culture), on the other hand, what cries, what laments and what exclamations of jubilation! Emotions expressed almost in their pure state. We go from one extreme to another: from revolt to thanksgiving, from anxiety to adoration, from repentance to joy. Even the most secret human passions are exposed to broad daylight.

Be Authentic

Speaking of these "hidden passions," do you, like the psalmist, feel able to proclaim them to the face of the Lord? Are you able to consider him as the Friend, the Bridegroom, the Intimate One before whom you may lay open your heart? And will you dare accuse him of being the Friend who seems to have abandoned you, the Bridegroom who has betrayed you, the Intimate One who no longer responds? I am thinking here of all that is bitterness and resentment against God, feelings of injustice on his part towards you, even your anger with him because you consider him responsible for what is happening to you.

> I use the whole range of my usual vocabulary (someone answers the question: "Do you have favorite words?" during an inquiry on prayer). It goes from the warmest thank you to Cambrone's word … which sometimes escapes me, even when I am praying.[13]

Many faithful do not dare. They are full of animosity towards God throughout the whole day, but when they set about to pray at the end of the day, they hide their face behind a mask of pious neutrality because they say:

"We cannot say such things to the Lord."

"Why, yes, you can."

"I am praying, I must have the right dispositions."

"In fact, you don't. Those you claim you have are not really your own."

"They are ones I would like to have and which I am asking him to give me."

"Meanwhile, you are not the one praying. The person you think you should be is."

You need to be bold to a certain degree to tell God that you are angry with him. If this can reassure you, tell yourself that, since the days of Job, he can take a lot. It is not a matter of lacking respect for the Most High, but of proving that you live intensely enough with him not to try to keep anything hidden from him. In any case, just try to hide something from him …

> One day, when I was most disappointed about not receiving something I was so eager to have, I begrudged God. I was so angry with him that I refused to speak and pray to him for two whole days. You will say that this was childish of me. But it was very effective. Deep down in my heart, I knew I could trust God enough to tell him about my resentment, as I am in the habit of doing with my friends. I am not afraid of expressing my negative feelings to them because I know they love me enough to understand.[14]

Do not worry about the violent nature of your language. Feeling compelled to conceal these negative feelings would be much more disturbing, for this would be a sign that you cannot deal with God in any other way but with courtesy, "as we treat acquaintances rather than intimate friends."[15] Carrying on insignificant chat in proper language.

It is only by expressing them, and not by repressing them, that you may gradually rid yourself of these feelings. He will take no offense, you may be sure. Once again, he will be learning nothing new. He will even see there a proof of trust on your part. When you are able to express (I was going to say "serenely," but let us rather say "honestly") your anger to someone else, is this not a sign that you feel comfortable with that person? Not when you lose control of yourself, which is something else, but when you are able to share the emotion you feel. If you have only a superficial, fragile and unsure relationship with that person, you will not take the risk of revealing your resentment freely, for fear of losing the little friendship he has for you. If you are sure of his kindly attitude towards you, or of the stability of your mutual bond, you will have the boldness and the honesty to tell him that you hold a grudge against him. "The opposite of love is not anger, or even hatred, it is being cold and indifferent."[16]

I am convinced that the Lord, from whom nothing is hidden, would prefer to see you in a furious but honest state against him, rather than full of respect, but stiff and fretting from a distance. Again, think of Job's friends.

Know That He Answers You, Even If ...

When I speak to people who are taking their first steps in prayer, I tend to warn them against certain expressions that may lead to confusion when defining their relationship with God. For example, "conversing with God," "conversation with God," or, more boldly, "dialogue." I use them myself, of course, since I cannot do otherwise, knowing that those used to prayer will make the necessary modifications. But a word like "dialogue," when applied to our relationship with God, would imply that he replies to us in the same tone as the one we use to speak to him. This would be, just the same, something of an illusion.

I would not insist on this point, it is so obvious, if I did not meet some faithful sometimes who, being eager to make progress in their journey to God, complain that, in their prayers, "all they do is speak, and that they do not know how to listen." They have the impression that their own wordiness takes so much space that God has little chance to make himself heard.

Fine, up to here. "Listen, Israel," the prophets, after all, repeat a hundred times.

They then decide to try to be more silent and "to listen" better to whatever the Lord would wish to tell them.

I always agree.

To do this, they interrupt their monologue and strain their ear the best they can … and are disappointed that they hear nothing. Or rather, they hear all sorts of things. As soon as they try to be somewhat silent, this silence is filled with distractions and phantasmagoria of all kinds, noises, brawls, and speeches. These come from everywhere except heaven.

"So God does not wish to speak? Or does he have nothing to tell you?"

Then the great question comes up necessarily.

"What do I do that is not right?"

"Why, nothing. Except that, normally, God does not speak to us in this way."

Let us first admit that God is not talkative. We want to believe that God spoke to Moses, that saints heard "voices"; but for us, the unqualified, who have no ecstasies, would it not be a pious exaggeration to claim that God speaks to us? Is this not … a manner of speaking?

Let us then admit that he probably has his own ways of making his thoughts understood. He has neither lips, nor a throat to emit sounds that we could "hear." He must then go about this in some other way.

Finally, we must acknowledge that he has only one thing to tell us, that he loves us. But when this word comes from him, it is too rich in meaning to be contained in one sentence. Therefore, he will make it known to us in a much more mysterious fashion.

His way of making himself heard goes by way of this famous depth of heart. "When you search for me, you will find me; if you seek me with all your heart, I will let you find me" (*Jer* 29:13-14). Did not Teresa of Avila write the following on this subject to her Carmelite sisters: "Do you suppose that because we cannot hear him, he is silent? He speaks clearly to the heart when we beg him from our hearts to do so."[17]

If he speaks to the heart, then, logically, the heart must be attentive. We could then say that God's response is more "felt" than "heard." This does not mean that God speaks to our moods but that his answer often comes through, especially in the beginning, by what human beings experience in prayer. If the depths of the heart are a kind of "spiritual organism," experience teaches us that this person is gifted with "spiritual senses."[18] God speaks to these spiritual senses and they are first able to perceive him.

It is not a voice that we can hear, coming from elsewhere. It is a presence that is sensed and manifested within.

If this is so, God would speak to us, not through our external senses, but by making his presence felt by the alert heart. Feelings of *gentleness and joy, of calm and serenity*, those are the elements of his "response." "God speaks to the heart … in utmost peace and tranquillity, so that the

soul may listen and hear the words of the Lord t
when in this secret place he speaks this peace."[19]

To one who has no experience of this, that may seem to be completely irrational, as incomprehensible as the taste of an apple to one that has never had a bite of one. Whole treatises would not be enough to give a precise idea of its taste: only tasting the fruit will enable us to know. But whoever has already done so, be it ever so slightly, (here, one of the five senses, as by chance) will detect the presence of God.

The problem is not that God is silent but that *we are deaf*. We are constantly on the surface of our being. We lose ourselves in trifles. We nourish our superficial mirages. But the one whose heart is enkindled by a loving conversation with the Bridegroom ultimately senses at what depths he must listen and hear.

> Congratulations for your happy return home. After being away, home is a paradise. Everyone feels this in the same way. We experience exactly the same thing when, after a distraction, we come back to attention and interior life. When we are in the heart, we are at home; when we are not there, we are homeless. And this is, above all, what we must be concerned about.[20]

The mechanism at work is quite simple. If, as we have seen, you have prayed to God with the feelings of your heart, exposing to him all that dwells in you on the deepest emotional level possible, gradually your ability to sense him will become polarized on the same level. You will center yourself on this level. That is where your consciousness will be set. It is there as well that God "speaks" to you. Both of you will be on the same wavelength.

On the contrary, if you act like the fiancée who is satisfied with sharing with her betrothed only the details about the color of the wallpaper in the bedroom, do not expect too much … If, when you pray to God, you speak of philosophy and metaphysics (fascinating, is it not? …), he will have nothing to say in reply since what he would like to communicate to you concerns your interior life. And if he ever tries to do this, your emotional center, its spiritual senses being dead and inactive, will hear nothing since you are totally focused on your own gray matter.

Go Back to Your Heart

This is an essential theme in the Bible. It constantly is taken up again in the monastic tradition, particularly in the Cistercian one. The elders relentlessly repeated this advice, "Go back to your heart," to the novices. This has been relentlessly taught as well by the spiritual masters of the Eastern Churches to all who want to learn to pray. Do they not speak of the prayer of the heart?

> Recollect yourselves and try not to leave your heart, for the Lord is found there. Strive to achieve this, work at it. When you reach this state, you will understand how precious it is.[21]

If you try to approach God to enter into a relationship with him, you will not know straightaway *how* and *where* this encounter should take place. After the first tentative efforts, often fruitless, you will gradually go down into your depths. An important aspect of this maturing process will consist in this discovery of – or in sensing only – the interior organ that allows you to be in touch with God.

Come the day when you succeed in going down to these depths, it will be easy for you to take the last step to your interior Host. He will be there "one prayer's throw away," if you allow me to use this expression.

> We then experience an astonishing paradox: it is by going down to our uttermost depths that we come out of ourselves in the surest way! Indeed, to penetrate into the caverns of the heart is to venture beyond the superficial self, into the secret chamber, the Holy of Holies, the tabernacle of the reunion where the ineffable encounter with the Beloved takes place. In this case, as St. Augustine says, "to enter is to come out, to climb, to descend."[22]

For someone who is not yet familiar with this region of his being, the best route to approach it is that of *affectivity*. Not the totally superficial sensitivity, but the profound impulse of love. "Express your feelings," "display your true emotions before him," "ask him to reach your buried desires …" Why so much insistence on my part on the affective dimension of your conversation with God, if not to hollow out your heart down to its very core? "Where is the heart? It is where you feel sadness, joy, anger and other emotions. Remain attentive there […] Dwell in your heart, firmly believing that God, too, is there."[23]

Listen to the Silence

Here you are down in your heart. You have reached that level by following the feelings coming out of it, against the grain, like one of Ariadne's threads. This is the first step.

"Focus your attention on the interval of silence between your sentences," I then said. Why? This short interval of silence still resounds with the emotion you have just expressed, does it not? Does not the glowing enthusiasm of the senses still echo within you even if the expression of it is ended? So, *you are in the profound depths of your heart, but without uttering a word. Only listening.* You are at the core of your own being and able "to listen to" what echoes from there. Another step taken …

As we have seen, the content of the heart goes beyond the content of the words that strive to express it through our conversations. The third phase consists in becoming aware that there is a message there which, although it cannot be expressed, is nonetheless communicated. We have seen this when we considered the examples of contacts between neighbors, the father-son relationship and those of friendship. A surplus of meaning circulates between the persons speaking, is caught on both sides, but is not emitted or perceived in the form of words. Something not said, surely, but how expressive!

An exchange between lovers is the perfect type of this, being composed almost exclusively from the abundance of meaning. Any lover is aware of that: he will never manage to "say" this meaning. The more he tries to do so, the less he succeeds.

And now, what about prayer in all that? But, good heavens … so is prayer an exchange of love … It expresses itself perfectly in this eloquent silence … It is expressed through language, for it cannot do otherwise, but it is not part of it. It is always beyond it.

Here on your part, you want him to know your love. But words escape and only "silence" can attempt to "say" it. Only silence can manage to reveal your love for God. I was urging you, a few moments ago, to expose to him your experience, but *especially* to repeat to him that you love him (or at the very least that you want to love him). Why that? Because the language of love is the one that gives rise to the greatest abundance of meaning, the one most apt to create the silence you are seeking.

On his part, "God has nothing else to say except his love for you," as we have said. If love sometimes lets itself "be heard" in words, it especially lets itself be "sensed" beyond the words.

Moreover, since God speaks without emitting any sounds, he can logically make himself heard only in this eloquent silence which is sometimes created between your sentences. That is why we have said clearly, it seems to me, that it is in the depths of the heart that God lets himself be sensed, for it is only there that silence becomes "indwelt." And last but not least, now that you are there "listening attentively," apt "to sense" him since you yourself have stopped speaking for a few fractions of a second, is to become attentive to what echoes within you.

So apparently, this profound heart seemed to be silent by intervals, as we believed we could notice, but in reality, this silence is totally indwelt by the echoes of your own sighs first, then by the declarations of love coming from the Beloved. The "profound heart" becomes a "mystical heart."

Finally, one last step. This emotional overabundance, always there from the moment we communicate with others, as a rule, is only of a mediocre intensity. But it can grow to the extreme in certain peak-experiences. The unutterable then becomes the most important part of the communication. Think of Coretta King. Sharing becomes a communion beyond words.

That is it! We have found it: that is what contemplative prayer is all about! Its stakes consist in broadening this silence with the Beloved more and more, in attempting to prolong it in time for more than the few seconds it usually lasts, in giving it density and depth.

Extending this silence is a sufficiently important challenge for us to devote the next three chapters to it.

Notes

[1] *The Complete Works of Saint Teresa of Jesus,* vol. 2, *Way of Perfection*, p. 125.

[2] Saint Ignace de Loyola, *Exercices Spirituels*, trans. by François Courel, S.J. (Bruges: Desclée de Brouwer, 1963), p. 47.

[3] For a somewhat technical overview of the question applied to prayer, see Louis-Marie Chauvet, "Liturgie et prière. Éléments de réflexion anthropologique, théologique et pastorale," *La Maison-Dieu*, n° 195, 1993, pp. 49-90.

[4] Giovanni Papini, *Histoire du Christ* (Paris: Payot, 1925), p. 445.

[5] In the Orthodox Churches, a staretz is a spiritual father (most of the time a monk) experienced in directing the beginners in the paths of the spiritual way.

[6] For example, *Ps* 37:6-9 or 41:5-9.

[7] Like sin in Psalm 51, the *Miserere*, or Psalm 130, *De profundis*.

[8] *Ps* 69:5; 3:1.

[9] *Ps* 43:1-3; 42:10; 56:2-8; 57:2-7.

[10] *Ps* 29:4.

[11] *Ps* 30:9-14.

[12] *Ps* 34. One sole exception that only confirms the rule, Psalm 107 in which four classes of tried-and-saved are called successively to the witness bar to give thanks.

[13] *Fêtes et saisons*, n° 326, June-July 1978, p. 24.

[14] Anthony de Mello, *Allez vers Dieu* (Montreal/Paris: Bellarmin/Desclée de Brouwer, 1997), p. 91.

[15] *Ibid.*, p. 91.

[16] *Ibid.*, p. 92.

[17] *The Complete Works of Saint Teresa of Jesus*, vol. 2, *Way of Perfection*, p. 103.

[18] Since the beginning of the Christian experience, especially since St. Augustine (who said, "Bring me a lover and he will *feel* what I am say-

ing"), we speak of the soul as having senses corresponding to our physical senses. These enable us to "see" the invisible presence of God, to "taste" his ineffable savor, to "touch" his impalpable action, to "breathe" his unparalleled gentleness. Therefore, to "listen" also to his inaudible answer. Cf. Karl Rahner, "Les débuts d'une doctrine des cinq sens spirituels chez Origène," *Revue d'ascétique et de mystique*, n° 13, 1932, pp. 113-145; *id.*, "La doctrine des sens spirituels au Moyen Âge, en particulier chez S. Bonaventure," *RAM*, n° 14, 1933, pp. 263-299.

[19] *The Complete Works of Saint John of the Cross*, vol. 3, *Living Flame of Love*, p. 162.

[20] Theophane the Recluse, quoted in Igumen Chariton of Valaam, *op. cit.*, p. 264.

[21] *Ibid.*, p. 267.

[22] Daniel Maurin, *L'oraison du cœur. Un chemin vers Dieu* (Paris/Fribourg: St. Paul Editions, 1993), p. 142.

[23] Theophane the Recluse, quoted by Igumen Chariton of Valaam, *op. cit.*, p. 262.

3

… murmuring a word to him

"Love has but one word,
and while it is always saying it,
it never repeats it."
Lacordaire

The setting sun is lightening up the summer evening. The air is not absolutely cool, but there is no longer the humidity of a few days ago.

Hector and Amelia are in their rocking chairs on the veranda, taking advantage of the last evenings before the autumn already heralded by one or another leaf of the maple tree in the yard. He has brought his cane, she, her perpetual embroidered cape. Both of them have come to the stage in life when people may take the liberty of astonishing their guests by having them guess their age.

"And almost nine months …" is pointed out.

But when they are alone, as they are now, silence reigns between them, a silence that goes on and on without ever being heavy.

"You don't happen to feel cold …?" Hector inquires, very gently, without seeming to, between two cries from the birds.

"You don't happen to feel cold?" Is it possible for him to come up with a more trivial question? Nothing to say that is more pleasant, more passionate after so many years?

Still, what we are not aware of is that Amelia has always been somewhat sensitive to the cold, even if she refuses to admit it. She will admit this all the less since she knows that her little old man loves to stay out in his rocking chair. But, while preferring to stay out for some time yet, Hector knows that his little old lady is quite sensitive to the cold, and that perhaps she would prefer to go indoors. But she will not ask to do this on her own. He knows that as well. Amelia well knows that her old man knows that she suffers from the cold. In turn, old Hector knows very well that his old lady knows that he knows that she is sensitive to the cold. And the good little old lady knows that her little old man knows that …

"You don't happen to feel cold?" As arch-trivial as it is, the expression takes on its full meaning. Living together for fifty years, getting to know each other and being attentive to each other for as many years. This is a whole life of mutual tender love. All of it summed up, condensed in five words. Five words that mean everything, something that could mislead us. A little bit of a sentence about nothing at all that says so many things. It sums up a whole life of love.

One or Two Words That Say Everything

The first stages of prayer are marked by a certain amount of verbosity. Your spiritual attitudes vary and you abound in words. Then an inevitable process of simplification sets it. You move gradually from the display of a multitude of feelings before God (faith, trust, hope, surrender, love) to a more global attitude. To a much simpler one. Your life with God, which until now has shimmered in all sorts of facets, becomes more and more simple and unified.

Personally, after a few years spent in the monastery, every time I succeeded in having a prayerful attitude of a certain depth, I realized that it was always the same overall spiritual attitude that enlivened me. With a few variations at times.

This does not mean being impoverished. On the contrary. It is even a charisma in every great spiritual master. St. Augustine could have summed up his quest, nonetheless rich and complex, with the "Love of the Beautiful and the True" and everything would have been said. St. Francis of Assisi with "Espousing Lady Poverty." St. Bernard of Clairvaux with "The Love of the Bridegroom." St. Thérèse of Lisieux with "The Little Way of Trust." And each one in doing this held the Gospel in its entirety, as when we take hold of a corner of the tablecloth and pull on it firmly. We are pulling only a corner of it, but nevertheless the whole tablecloth follows and so does everything on it.

St. Agnes, the young Roman martyr, who was only twelve, used only two words to reply to her executioners: "*Amo Christum.*" *Amo Christum*: I love Christ. All her sense of Christianity was summed up in this exclamation.

Find your own spiritual attitude. Express it in a short formula that sums it up. That expresses what you *experience* with God when you pray. Use an excerpt from a psalm, two words from the Gospel. An expression that says everything you want to tell him. No, more than that: all that you feel like being, like becoming before him. What would I want to be for him? What would I like God to become for me …? Expressed in two words.

A Word to Sustain Prayer

The moment you have set for yourself to encounter God in prayer has come. You withdraw a little by yourself, in a quiet corner and, why not, a corner which is set up for that. You kneel down, or you sit back on your heels, or on a chair, a cushion or again on a small prayer stool, no matter. If you are not yet relaxed enough, begin by calming down your breathing.

Then, from the start, repeat your little formula, every time you breathe out in a calm and poised way. Breathe out gently while murmuring it, and as you breathe in again, let it echo within you. All this in a profound peace, without thinking too much of your breathing. Let yourself be borne by the content of what you are saying. Do this ten, twelve, fifteen times until you feel that you are somewhat in the presence of God.

This initial repetition, slow but continuous, to the rhythm of your breathing, has a twofold objective. First, it must help you to accomplish, but this time on the mental level, what you have already tried to do on the physical level by withdrawing yourself from your daily life. Break away from your previous occupations. Set aside what you were doing in order to do something else. Change the course of your concerns and the current of your thoughts. And, secondly, to put yourself in the presence of the Most High.

That is, for a set length of time, you strive to be focused on him alone by speaking to him through your short formula.

Once you have made this transition, once you sense his presence, you may stop repeating your formula, you do not need it any more. It becomes superfluous because you have reached your objective: meeting him. Basically, your formula is a dart you have shot several times with a precise purpose: to allow an encounter with God. Once the goal is reached, shooting the dart again would amount to useless fretting. Remain in this silence in which God allows himself to be apprehended. Be still, do nothing, stay within the range of his radiance, savor his presence.

> The most we should do is, occasionally, and quite gently, to utter a single word, like a person giving a little puff to a candle, when he sees it has almost gone out, so as to make it burn again; though, if it were fully alight, I suppose the only result of blowing on it would be to put it out. I think the puff should be a gentle one because, if we begin to tax our brains by making up long speeches, the will may become active again.[2]

If the short formula is whispered attentively and sincerely, it will be followed by a certain *interior resonance*. Immediately after the word, without repeating it, it continues to resound within you like an echo in a hallway. Or like a chord on the organ which, even if the organist's fingers have left the keys, keeps on reverberating in a decrescendo in the arches of the cathedral vault. Let your little word reverberate within you as long as possible. That is where the purest prayer lies, in this silence that is still resonant.

This indwelt silence, without any repetition, in ordinary people like you and me, will on average last two or three seconds, measured with watch in hand. If you are in a phase of great fervor, five seconds. If you are ever granted exceptional gifts of contemplation, something exceedingly rare, ten seconds.

As a rule, after two or three seconds of "emptiness" in the intellect, some distraction will present itself. It may be any digressions of the mind coming to take up the vacant space. If you let it come in and settle down, if you start to dialogue with it, you will no longer be able to rid yourself of it. At least, it will not be easy. It is better to reject it *before* it settles down in you. How? By going back to your little formula as soon as you see the distraction coming. Once or twice. A simple recall is enough since there is no true break to make and the feeling of the presence of God has not yet totally disappeared. Just something to stay on course. Again this loving silence for two seconds. A silence soon threatened by another distraction that will have to be rejected again with the help of two or three repetitions. And so on to the end of the set time.

Consider the image of a bird of prey perched on the branch of a tree. As soon as it flies, to soar up in height, it beats its wings steadfastly. It is the starting point of prayer and the constant repetition of the beginning. Then, when it has reached a certain altitude, our bird becomes almost motionless, wings outspread, borne by the rising air currents. This is the short pause when the impulse of love bears you silently. If it loses altitude ever so slightly, two or three flutters of its wings will be enough to raise it again to the proper level. Like a distraction that tends to bring you down, one or two repetitions will be enough to raise you up again.

The objective, not always reached, far from it, is simply *this most calm and peaceful silence*, where nothing seems to happen, but where *God lets himself be sensed.*

Sometimes it will be useful to bring the session to an end in a little more formal way: one or two expressions of thanks for the graces received or regrets for having neglected to remain attentive.

The Mental and the Affective

What is going on when we are praying in this way?[3] Simply put, we could say that the human being is divided into two zones. There is first, on a high level, the rational zone, that of reflection and thought. Let us call it the *mental* zone. Then there is, let us say on a lower level, the zone of moods, of sensitivity and emotions which we call the *affective* zone.

These are two zones, to be sure, but they are closely interrelated. For example, if I have pleasant ideas, optimism and beautiful projects in my *mental* zone, these positive thoughts will be the kind that will provide agreeable emotions like pleasure, joy, serenity or enthusiasm in my *affectivity.* On the other hand, if, in my *mental* zone, I brood over gloomy thoughts and if I have regrets or fears, I will experience unpleasant emotions like sadness, guilt, anger or depression in my *affectivity.* In the end, *thoughts* and *emotions* mutually condition each other. Or more precisely, we *feel what we think.*

Love develops its most intense resonance at the deeper levels of the *affective* zone. In the depths of the heart. It is enough for the *mental* to think of the beloved; the emotion of love will follow. Since to pray is to love, it will be the same for prayer. Prayer comes first from the *affective* and preferably from the deeper levels.

However we almost always place prayer spontaneously in the *mental* zone. Praying is making a speech to God, we tell ourselves, a rational speech, well structured and well organized.

"Am I making too many requests? Do I say enough prayers of thanksgiving?"

We are concerned about the intellectual content.

"I am all distractions, I cannot pray."

Understand: "I have *ideas* that overtake me, that have no relation to the *ideas* I ought to have in a prayer that respects its rules." In short, praying would mean having proper ideas, but alas, "I have all kinds of *other ideas* that go through my head."

I agree that this may be most embarrassing, but are we really down to the root of the problem? Do we not pray with the heart? Still, if you complain about this to someone, what advice will this person invariably give you?

"*Think* more of God and of his love for you. Chase away these distractions mercilessly. *Concentrate* … In other words, 'Set prayer well in your head.'"

If prayer resides in the *affective* zone, as we have seen, one idea emerging in the *mental* zone does not perturb it as such, but because of the correlation between the two zones, it runs a high risk of taking over my *affective* zone. Then, goodbye to the presence of God. There lies the problem of distractions. Not that they "go through my head," but that they end up entering my heart.

You have set about to pray. The quiet repetition has calmed you down and put you more or less in the presence of God. Then, almost inevitably, there rises in your head some project dear to you, or a personal or professional concern that has been gnawing at you for some time. You will have to give proof of great determination if you do not want the emotional whirlwinds to disturb your interior calm. This will be almost inevitable, always because of the correlation between the two zones.

"The solution is very simple," you will say. "Preventing the mind machine from operating would be enough."

Illusion. The *mental* zone is always at work: impossible to stop it. It even works at nighttime. And even then, it has an influence on my *affective* zone. Indeed, when I have beautiful dreams in the first, I feel calm and serene in the second, and, inversely, when I have nightmares, I wake up with a start, in anguish. In spite of myself, I will always have some thoughts trotting in my head; these will inevitably influence my emotional existence.

Applying This to Meditation

Almost all the techniques of meditation are based on this psychological pattern. Let us take a very simple case: that of transcendental meditation. What do people say as they meditate?

You sit in such and such a way and you are given a *mantra* that you must repeat without interruption. You must reject any thought that has nothing to do with your *mantra* and you firmly concentrate on the latter. As soon as a distraction comes up, you chase it away by repeating your *mantra* again. As soon as you realize that you are scattered or gone elsewhere, you come back to your *mantra*. Do that throughout your whole thirty minutes of meditation.

Now the *mantra* given to the one meditating consists in a formula that has no meaning whatsoever, an expression that means nothing. Most of the time, it is made up of a sound to emit or of an onomatopoeia which is supposed to resemble all the possible sounds, OOUMM, for example. What happens then?

The *mental* zone of the one meditating, for lack of being able to be completely still, is forced to focus on an object of no content.

> Our intellect needs to be busy at something. Our understanding is like the trump of an elephant opening a procession along a narrow street cluttered with market stalls. If the trump is not busy, it explores this side and that side and rummages here and there. But it suffices to give it something as simple as a bamboo branch to hold with its trump for the elephant to open the way and its trump straightens out and is perfectly stable. We cannot expect our intellectual faculties to remain quiet; to be active is part of their nature. That is why we give them a word or a simple formula to keep them busy.[4]

The role of repetition is to disconnect the thinking mind from its usual operations. In other words, the imagination, the mad cap of our minds, is set on neutral. It idles away (almost) all its fuel. If this is put to work carefully, the result will be that the *affective* will, in turn, be set in neutral since it no longer receives any material from the *mental* zone. A great calm from beginning to end.

This is not prayer since there is not an encounter with God as yet, but it is greatly beneficial to many people. In this over-excited, maddening, nerve-wracking and tense world in which we live, it helps certain people to stop simply, to remain still, to do nothing and to think of nothing.

To savor this beneficial emptiness, one or two half-hours a day.

You have already noticed the word *mantra* to designate the short formula used. Etymologically speaking, the word comes from the Sanskrit root *man* that refers to the intellect, and from the suffix *tra* which means tool or utensil. The *mantra* is therefore a *mental tool* we use for a precise purpose in the production of thoughts. Or, as is the case here, in the restraint and control of thoughts.

Here the instrument we use consists in a repeated word. There are many others. Spiritual masters of all religions have developed a whole repertory of them.

Here are a few examples. Focus your attention on an imaginary spot right in the center of the head. On a spot located exactly between the eyes. Or on the navel. In the palm of the hands. Concentrate on a black spot painted on a white sheet of paper stuck on the wall.[5] On the flame of a candle.

The procedure is always the same: every time you catch yourself thinking about something else, go back invariably to the object chosen to concentrate uniquely on it. And the result sought is always the same: reducing the intellect to stillness in order to make the whole interior self become still.

For some decades, meditation centers for Christian believers have been formed; they have adopted this same psychological pattern as their basis.

In one of these centers, the School of Christian Meditation, organized by John Main, O.S.B., and Lawrence Freeman, O.S.B., the word suggested and widely used is *maranatha*.[6]

On the one hand the word is of Biblical origin since the New Testament uses it twice. It seems to have been familiar enough to the first Christian communities so that neither Paul nor John felt the need to translate it for their readers. This confers upon it an unquestionable Christian dimension for us still today. Moreover, if we examine its meaning ("Come, Lord"), it constitutes a whole program for the one who, in the process of meditation, is in quest of God.

But, in spite of that, this same word stills remains foreign to us, be it only because of its language. And I suspect that for most Christians, even the well informed, this word bears no affective overtones. We have to perform some intellectual gymnastics to make the content of this word touch us in the depths of our hearts. This is not impossible, of course, but neither is it spontaneous. But this neutrality is precisely the effect deliberately sought for: "Since this is an Aramaic word, it conjures up in us only a few associations or mental images and we are all the less inclined to reflect on its meaning when we use it."[7]

To illustrate this, we must turn our attention away from the meaning of the mantra or from ideas it suggests to listen only to its sound. Fr. Main relates the adventure of an honest Irish woman who presented herself at one of his prayer groups. The procedure was explained to her and she was taught the usual mantra. The good lady listened to the instructions and all those present went on to meditate. But as she walked into the room, she forgot the mantra. She sat down and wondered how she could even meditate without the mantra. "But, Father, God is good! The word came back to me after a few moments: *Maccoshla, Maccoshla!*"[8]

Another characteristic of the method suggested by the School of Christian Meditation is the instruction to say the word from the beginning to the end of the period without interruption. This is according to the logic of things. If the suggested word (*maranatha),* from its language and, at least partially, from its content, has no dimension of love, it will conjure up nothing new on the level of the *affective* zone. If by chance, an interior silence emerges, it will be barren. We will feel "good." But no more. It will be a silence that is not indwelt, but rather empty.

Not only is this silence unsought for, but when it comes, it must not be nourished for it is the opposite of the pedagogy of the initiative.

> Sometimes, while praying the word, we may experience a certain level of quietude and calm, and we may be tempted to say to ourselves: that is fine. I think I will set aside my mantra and simply savor this experience. Then we are the oarsman who leaves the shore of the river to cross over to the other side. Once he is in the water, he feels the sun warming his back. "How pleasant," he says. "I think I will lay down my oars, stretch out in the boat and relax for a while." He falls asleep and, when he wakes up, he discovers that the current has carried him away, very far from his goal. The purpose of the discipline of relentlessly repeating the word from the beginning to the end of the meditation is to make us cross the river, to make us move from the shore of self-concern to that of union with the consciousness of Christ.[9]

People trained in this school quite regularly come to me for advice.

"I have practiced this form of meditation faithfully for years. At first, it helped me a great deal to calm down, to enter into myself. But for some time, I have had the sensation of going around in circles. I do not have the impression of encountering God. Worse, I do not even have the impression of praying. There I am. All I do is concentrate."

I do not claim that this way cannot lead to God.[10] This is probably the case for many … but these people do not come to me to get them out of their predicament … I claim still less to know a way that will lead unfailingly to God. But I tell myself that I must nonetheless put all the odds on our side and avoid making a hurdle race out of prayer. If it means to love, let us act like lovers …

A Word Making the Heart Pray

Like them, there will come a time when all you have to tell him can be summed up in two words. Then you will not feel like becoming involved in a complicated scheme, or like following well-organized procedures, whether a method of prayer, a psalm or another text prepared ahead of time.

> When you pray, do not attempt to speak a great deal for fear that your mind may be distracted by the search for words. One sole word from the publican appeased God and one sole cry of faith saved the good thief. Loquacity in prayer often disperses the mind, fills it with images, whereas the repetition of the same word usually puts it to silence.[11]

If contemplative prayer consists mainly in lengthening the intervals set between words, would not the simplest way be to reduce the time taken by these words?

We do not achieve pure prayer by adding but by cutting off, not by accumulating thoughts but by simplifying them. Speak little from the mouth but much from the heart.

Everything can be contained in two or three words that are enough for you to go back to, with short intervals of silence, letting the words echo in your heart. Think more of him than of the words you are saying.

Objective

Even if you have to dwell on the question, the most important thing is not the word and its content, nor the rhythm of its repetition; *it is the silence between*. And the trick is to make this silence affectionate, loving, filled with the encounter. The invocation is only a springboard to this silence. This *full silence, indwelt by the presence* is the objective.

We all have been aware, at one time or another, that sometimes there are moments when the words of prayer seem to slip away and leave us in an interior silence. It would seem as if words disturb this tranquility. But then we hasten to pick up the thread of our prayer, thinking we are under the effect of dozing. We readily admit we are guilty of distractions. And still ... If we agree to slip away into this silence without putting up any resistance, we discover a *presence*. It manifests itself in our consciousness, still unknown, perhaps blurred, indistinct, at times disturbed by interfering thoughts. Yet a silent recollection settles in. A feeling of peace spreads in our being in an unexpected way: such a pleasant state that we hold back our breath spontaneously so as not to disturb this peace. Any word, any movement would be like an inner wrenching; in silence, we savor this *something* that is indescribable and yet so real.

We see nothing. There is no one we can touch or hear distinctly. Still, something, or rather *Someone* manifests himself beyond the words, and if we let him have his way, we enter into his intimacy.

Once the quietude has been achieved, do not be concerned any more about the method. *Let Christ seize you!* For this is he. And *you are in the depths of your heart!*

Content

If we give a bamboo stick to an elephant, he will walk straight on. Suppose we gave him a bag of peanuts instead. Would he go rummaging everywhere? Still less than with his bamboo branch. Would he not saunter in a yet straighter path? The aroma of the peanuts would even make him trot happily, I am sure. Straight on.

As opposed to the School of Christian Meditation, I think it is imperative that the formula should hold an expressive content. It may vary infinitely from one person to the next, but one is needed. Not a meaningless expression that we could pick up by chance in a telephone directory. Nor one that we could choose in a Sanskrit dictionary producing a fine exotic resonance. Pity! The ideal would be to find a name for God that would suit your relationship with him, a name that would describe what he is for you and what you are for him.

The story is told about a good old parish priest who, with age, had developed a prayer in familiar, almost naïve terms. At the end of the Sunday Eucharist, after the communion rite, he would sit in the celebrant's chair and obviously make his act of thanksgiving. As he had become somewhat hard of hearing with the years, he sometimes did what many people do in his condition: he would mumble aloud under his breath. Since he did not hear himself, he thought that no one else did either. One fine day, there happened what was bound to happen: the microphone was left on. So the whole assembly could hear him muttering, throughout the whole church: "My God, my all …" a loud breath, then: "The hell with the rest …"

You will not have to rack your brain to find the short formula suitable for you, it is already present in your own depths. When we love someone, we do not go searching in a large dictionary of quotations for the well-styled sentence that will express perfectly what we feel. This will spring up by itself.

> If you don't have much to tell me
> Write the words "I love you" a hundred times.
> This will be the most beautiful poem.
> A hundred times a hundred is not much
> For those who love each other.[12]

It may be a very trite expression, but it is *your own*. It is rich in meaning because you are experiencing it. It becomes unique because *you* are the one saying it.

If it is rather long, divide it into two or three breaths. Feel very free, follow your own path and remain very flexible. Nothing systematic, but the freedom of the one who loves.

St. Thérèse of the Child Jesus wrote that when she was near the tabernacle, she could say only one thing: "My God, you know that I love you" and she felt that this prayer, so banal, did not weary Jesus.

In the fifth century, after spending seven years in the Egyptian desert to initiate himself into the spiritual experience of the great monks of the Eastern Church, John Cassian came back to settle in Marseilles to found two monasteries. That is where he transmitted to the Western Church what he had received from the famous Fathers of the Desert. Speaking, among other things, about repetitive prayer, he gave as a model this "humble verse": "O God, deliver me. O Lord, make haste to help me" (*Ps* 70:1). His teaching had such an influence on the Western Church that, still today, every liturgical hour of the Roman breviary begins with this little excerpt from a psalm.[13]

Another monk of the same period used the prayer: "Lord, what you will, when you will."

You are probably familiar with the expression used in the Orthodox Church: "Lord Jesus Christ, Son of the living God, have mercy on me, a sinner." This is a combination of two texts from the Gospel: the cry of the blind man of Jericho, "Jesus, Son of David, have mercy on me" (*Lk* 18:38) and the prayer of the publican, "God, be merciful to me, a sinner!" (*Lk* 18:13). It was made popular in the Western World by *The Way of a Pilgrim*.[14]

This expression is part of a very long tradition and holds great richness in doctrine,[15] but for practical purposes, personally, I find that it is perhaps a little long. Fourteen words in English, only seven in Greek and Russian.[16] It seems preferable therefore to subdivide it in three parts, with a short pause between each. Repeat slowly and without effort: "Lord Jesus Christ / Son of the living God / have mercy on me." Or the abridged version: "Lord Jesus, have mercy."

You may also opt for another traditional expression of the Eastern liturgy, the Trisagion, and divide it again in three parts: "Holy God, mighty God / immortal God / have mercy on us."

Or from the psalms. "My rock and my fortress" (*Ps* 31:3). Not heartwarming enough, it makes shivers run down your back … Let us try something else: "Lord, you are my refuge" (*Ps* 31:4). Or again: "Let your steadfast love, O Lord, be upon us [me]" (*Ps* 33:22). Already better …

You may adopt the exclamation of the apostle Thomas: "My Lord and my God" (*Jn* 20:28). Could we find anything still more heartwarming? "Jesus I love you." Perfect … "Jesus, you love me." Still better.

"Abba, Father," if we are drawn more to the Father than to the Son. "Come, Holy Spirit," if we are turned to the Holy Spirit. Always act with freedom and flexibility.

"You loved me / You gave yourself for me" (*Gal* 2:20). Superb … Or again Peter's profession that is so beautiful: "Lord, you know everything, you know that I love you" (*Jn* 21:17). Or inspired by the Song of Songs: "I am my beloved's / and my Beloved is mine" (*Song* 6:3). Or simply: "Lord, abide in me." St. Francis of Assisi often exclaimed: "My God and my all." Our old parish priest took it up again … with some changes.

Personally, I have been using the same formula for years already. I have told myself many times that I should change. To avoid being caught up in the hum of routine. But every time I set about praying, the same one comes back to me. It is mine to such an extent now, and is so rich with experiences acquired with time. I would really like to change, but the Lord has granted me so many graces with that one … so what would be the use?

Jean Lafrance, a well-known French spiritual master who died recently, suggests, for his part, the following formulation: "Father / in Jesus' name / give me your Spirit."[17]

It is based in a wonderful way on the theology of the New Testament, although, in my opinion, it is somewhat long. It only needs to be subdivided.

But if you do not succeed in finding a short expression that suits you, do not rack your brain. Simply use the word "Father" or the name "Jesus." No need to look any further. "Jesus," "Jesus Christ," "Lord Jesus," "Sweet Jesus,"[18] "My Beloved," "My Savior," "My Love." The shortest ones are the best.

"Rabboni" (*Jn* 20:16), a name that Mary Magdalene addressed to Jesus, so intimate and personal, to the extent that the evangelist gave up trying to translate it. This cry was Mary Magdalene's whole being, her total love, her whole desire ... in one sole word.

Do as she did: find a little word that resonates in your being. By means of a very calm and measured murmur, put yourself in the presence of God. Once you are open to this presence, stop the repetition, stop all maneuvers and *remain still in this silence indwelt by him.* You have reached your goal. A few seconds. Go back gently to your repetition as soon as another thought filters into your mind.

Tempo

Is there a particular rhythm that should be respected? The almost absolute silence of all the authors and all the confused tendencies on this question already provide the answer: No.

Everywhere, there is only one recommendation: recite "slowly, gently, quietly." And "in silent recollection, no haste, naturally." The prayer may adopt the rhythm of breathing. This is useful but not obligatory. If this does not happen on its own, let it go.

If we examine this matter with a magnifying glass, we hardly learn anything more. The Russian bishop-monk Ignatius Brianchaninov (1807-1867) thinks that about half an hour is needed to recite the Jesus Prayer about a hundred times.[19] Some recite it more rapidly while others take longer. In *The Way of a Pilgrim*, the staretz advises the pilgrim to start by reciting the prayer three thousand times a day. Then six thousand times. And finally, twelve thousand times. After which the pilgrim stopped counting. This presupposes a rather rapid rhythm.

But the prayer is a vital act and must not degenerate into a mechanical movement. True love uses no metronome. It is enough for it to maintain a proper balance between the "prayer-word" and the "filled-silence" by avoiding two snags:

- If you keep your invocation always present in your mind, you remain "in your head."
- If you remain idle, you risk staying "suspended in a void."

The key therefore consists in going back to your little formula, gently and lovingly every time your mind begins flitting about. Without, for all that, clinging to it, in order to leave space for the One who is awaited … beyond all formulas.

> The movements of the tongue and the heart, during prayer are the keys. Then comes the entrance into the room. There the mouth and the lips become silent; thought, reason, mind […] and their supplications have but to remain silent for the Master of the house has come in.[20]

As soon as the Beloved lets his presence be felt, let the little word lose itself in silence. To be taken up again only when an intruding thought wants to capture you in its net.

The bird of prey would become exhausted if it beat its wings constantly. If it fell asleep in the sky, it would crash to the ground. Two extremes to be avoided. No violence, no power strokes. No laborious efforts to keep it constantly in the mind: knocking on the door does not mean forcing the lock! Besides, you cannot even open the door on this side. The more you push, the more tightly closed it is! The Lord alone can open it for you: "Everyone who asks receives, and everyone who searches finds, and for everyone who knocks, the door will be opened" (*Lk* 11:10). He does not say, "Break down the door." But neither does he say, "Once is enough." We must seek, invoke with perseverance.

Variations

The great advantage of this way of living your relationship with the Lord is that the formula will emerge again at other moments of the day. When you have a "puff of prayer" between two occupations. If you have prayed for several months with a precise expression and it is well anchored in you, your desire for God, coming up unexpectedly in an off-peak moment of your day, will formulate itself on its own by means of this short word. This is normal: it is part of your "holy history." It expresses you to God and it is through it that God expresses himself to you.

And when the task of always beginning over again becomes monotonous, see what you experience when you utter the name of Jesus. Change your attitude gradually, repeat the word with varied feelings.

Murmur it at the beginning with *anticipation*. Without saying, "Lord, I long for you," express this attitude of the heart in the way you recite his name. After a few minutes, repeat the same while changing your attitude a bit: with *trust*. Not reflecting on trust, this would be turning your prayer back into your head, but by another manner of murmuring his name. Let yourself go on trusting in him, savor, experience this security. Then, always only by your way of repeating the same name, move to *adoration*, to *gratitude*, to *surrender*. There are many ways of saying, "My dear, my pet, my bunny."

Once again, do not think of surrender or of thanksgiving. That would become again a matter for the brain. Prayer is not a brain matter, but an inclination of the heart. "It is not about thinking much but praying much." Repeating, with warmth, the name of the beloved, this is the secret of lovers. It is the secret of contemplation.

The more we love, the better we pray. Prayer is the heart's attention lovingly focused on him. The more loving the attention, the better the prayer. All the rest is useless wrapping.

Bonds with the Christian Tradition

Hector and Amelia, on their balcony, made us see that the love relationship, as it becomes deeper with time, makes us communicate more and more while we chatter less and less. This law of love may be applied to prayer. We come to the point of expressing everything while saying almost nothing. One word is enough.

We have seen that reducing the speech of the intellect to a simple *mantra,* because of a psychological structure common to all humans, is a fact that may be observed throughout the whole evolution of the great spiritual traditions. Techniques of concentration and of immersing ourselves into our own depths are not legion. They are all interrelated. The inner life of the human being functions in an identical way at all latitudes.

I do not have the means of going back over the history of prayer based on the repetition of a formula in a Christian context, in only a few pages. This study has been taken up elsewhere; I can only refer you to it, as much on the Orthodox side[21] as on that of the Western Church.[22]

I will limit myself to a few probes here and there.

I have already mentioned, as I presented the possible formulas, a few great Christian figures like Cassian, Thérèse of the Child Jesus and Francis of Assisi. I hasten to add Francis of Sales.[23] For him contemplative prayer is possible not only in monasteries or reserved for women religious and the clergy, but it is also a right and a duty for soldiers, domestic employees, ladies of the court and their servants, businessmen and their wives. Firmly convinced of this, he took their lifestyle into account and suggested to them what he called (before the word took on a pharmaceutical meaning) "pills of mental prayer." Or "ejaculatory prayers." As for example: "O Jesus, I love you"; "Jesus, my love and my help"; "O my Jesus." Three little "javelins" projected to God, these short, quick, intense prayers expressing brief impulses of the heart, are scattered throughout the activities of the day. They may be recited anywhere and at any time. In the bus, at work, in the garden and in the kitchen, while dressing up and when walking, during periods of insomnia or distress. When other forms of prayer have become difficult. An invitation, within anyone's reach, to nourish our active hours with praise, offering, and calls made in trust to maintain this bond of love and to undertake everything under the eye of God.

How could we not recall the Christian devotion of the litanies? The rhythmic repetition, most often in a collective form, alternating with a soloist, of a short invocation that manages to push its way within our being. This is the comfortable monotony that allows the intellect to be stilled as the litany progresses. The intellect being in a calmed state, we now know what happens: the affective zone, in turn, becomes unified around the precise feeling instilled in us by the litany. Feeling of repentance ("Have mercy"); feeling of praise and adoration ("Blessed are you"); of petition and humility ("Pray for us"). A feeling which, if we become an integral part of the process, will take ever greater possession of us.

Let us conclude finally with the rosary which, while reputed to be a prayer for the poor, nonetheless calls for a complex undertaking. Once again, the same basic process: a constant repetition. In the first half of each Ave, we find a series of biblical expressions drawn from the salutation addressed to Mary by the Angel Gabriel, then by Elisabeth[24] and, in the second part, a repeated request for prayer for us. Therefore, a progressive stillness of the *mental* zone bringing with it, as always, the establishment of the corresponding feeling in the *affective* zone: veneration for the Mother of God and trust in her intercession on our behalf.

But this time, the turn of the expression is richer and more meaningful: the meditation on a "mystery" is added. Tradition has divided them into three triptychs with five tableaux each: the joyous mysteries, the sorrowful mysteries and the glorious mysteries. Each evokes an episode, always of a moving nature, in the life of the Virgin Mary. A particular mystery is attached to each decade, most often of an evangelical kind, and the one praying is urged to "meditate" on it while he recites the Hail Marys. To visualize the scene. To be impregnated with it. To let himself be touched by it. And finally, to let himself be moved. The *mental* zone is thus busy with one and the same subject, contemplating the Blessed Virgin through two different, but complementary, channels: the vocalization of a formula and the visualization of a scene. The *affective* dimension has but to follow. The way is doubly indicated.

Finally, it is Jesus himself who teaches us the repetition. He gives us two precepts that are apparently contradictory: "Not to pray by accumulating words" and "Praying unceasingly." I know of only one way of applying these two opposite approaches: praying by constantly repeating the same words. Do you see any other solution?

Notes

[1] Lacordaire, *Vie de Saint Dominique*, chapter 6.

[2] *The Complete Works of Saint Teresa of Avila*, vol. 2, *Way of Perfection*, p. 130.

[3] Here I am borrowing from "cognitive psychology," or more precisely from the "rational-emotive therapy" of the American Albert Ellis. The idea that our pattern of thought may have a profound influence on our mood has been expressed by a certain number of philosophers throughout the last 2500 years. More recently, the cognitive concept of our emotions was explored in the writings of many psychiatrists and psychologists like Alfred Adler, Karen Horney, Arnold Lazarus and Aaron Beck to mention only a few. For the history of this movement, see Albert Ellis, *Reason and Emotions in Psychotherapy* (New York: Lyle Stuart, 1962). For a popular version available in French, see Lucien Auger, *S'aider soi-même. Une psychothérapie par la raison* (Montreal: Éditions de l'Homme, 1974).

[4] Thomas Ryan, *La méditation à la portée de tous* (Montreal: Bellarmin, 1998), p. 72.

[5] Illustration reproduced in Barbara J. Rogers, *In the Center: the Story of a Retreat* (Notre Dame, Indiana: Ave Maria Press, 1983).

[6] In fact, they are two Aramaic words which can be divided in different ways: *maran ata* ("The Lord is coming") or *marana ta* ("Come, Lord!"). We find the expression in 1 *Cor* 16:22 and *Rev* 22:20. If we go to the end of Revelation, we will be inclined to adopt the second translation and see there a liturgical formula used in the communities of the Early Church to manifest their eagerness for the Parousia.

[7] Thomas Ryan, *op. cit.*, pp. 71-72.

[8] John Main, *La méditation chrétienne. Conférences de Gethsémani* (Montreal: Benedictine Priory, 1985), p. 44.

[9] Thomas Ryan, *op. cit.*, p. 73.

[10] The use of the mantra, as it is taught in the movement called "*Centering prayer*," could be placed half-way between the position of the School of Christian Meditation (mantra with no emotional resonance, constant repetition) and the position of the prayer of the heart that I am developing here (a word with an emotional charge, repetition used uniquely to lead to silence, which is the goal aimed at). See the bibliography at the end of this book. According to this movement, the word is used first as a word of love ("Jesus," "Lord," "Love," "Father," "Abba," etc.) which will emerge spontaneously as a response to the interior Presence. And, secondly, the use of the sacred word will vary according to circumstances: we must resort to it to sustain love, to come back to the presence, to return to God present in the center of our being when we are distracted by another thought. But we reach the point of going beyond the word to enter into peace and silence, and then we must set it aside. So there are different ways of using the mantra. Each may find the one suited to him. There are many dwelling places in the house of our common Father (*Jn* 14:2).

[11] St. John Climacus, *L'échelle sainte* (Bellefontaine Abbey, 1987), p. 292.

[12] Georges Dor, *La Manic.*

[13] On this subject, see the second lecture by Abbot Isaiah in John Cassian, *Conférences*, introduction, latin version, translation and notes by Dom E. Pichery (Paris: Cerf, 1958), vol. 2, pp. 85-93.

[14] *The Way of a Pilgrim*, trans. by Helen Bacovcin (New York: Doubleday, Image, 1978).

[15] On this subject, see the section on the Jesus Prayer in the bibliography at the end of this book.

[16] Speaking of prayer in tongues, St. Paul writes in 1 *Cor* 14:19: "In church I would rather speak five words with my mind [...] than ten thousand words in a tongue." According to the traditional Orthodox exegesis, the five words referred to are: "Lord Jesus Christ, have mercy on me," since this expression is made up of exactly five words in Greek and Russian.

[17] Jean Lafrance, *Demeure en Dieu* (Montreal: Médiaspaul, 1995), pp. 240-250.

[18] A whole chapter ought to be written on the spirituality of the name of Jesus and its invocation throughout the centuries, particularly with St. Bernard of Clairvaux ("The name of Jesus is honey in the mouth, a melody in the ear, a song of joy in the heart," he says in *Sermon XV on the Song of Songs*) and St. Bernardino of Siena ("This glorious name is the honor of those who have faith, the science of those who teach, the strength of those

who labor, the support of those who falter," excerpt from *The Eternal Gospel*). More in Daniel Maurin, *op. cit.*, pp. 53-65.

[19] Bishop Kallistos T. Ware in the introduction to Igumen Chariton of Valaam, *L'art de la prière* (Bellefontaine Abbey, 1966), p. 40.

[20] St. Isaac the Syrian, *Patrologia Græca*, vol. 86, p. 811.

[21] See the bibliography at the end of this book, in the section concerning the Jesus Prayer.

[22] Most of the books listed in the bibliography under the title "Christian Meditation" include a historical section, with the most significant quotations. They start from John Cassian, go through medieval monasticism, present *The Cloud of Unknowing* from an anonymous English mystic of the fourteenth century, then the sudden halts brought on by the Protestant Reformation, the Enlightenment crisis, the Inquisition reaction, the crisis of Quietism. They culminate in the contemporary rediscovery, triggered as much by the challenge of the spiritual movement from the Far East as by a rereading of our own spiritual legacy.

[23] St. Francis of Sales, *Introduction to the Devout Life* (New York: Alba House, 1992).

[24] "Greetings, favored one! The Lord is with you" (*Lk* 1:28). "Blessed are you among women, and blessed is the fruit of your womb" (*Lk* 1:42).

4

... mutually gazing at each other

"The face of man
is malleable.
To be like Christ,
it is enough to gaze at length
at the One in whose likeness
we wish to be."[1]
Christian de Chergé

All these detours have taken us very far from the candlelight supper of our two lovers. Still, they are our source of inspiration. Let us move closer to them, on the tip of our toes.

Too late. They are no longer talking to each other. Indeed, they are still speaking to each other but only hinting at what they mean to say. Still less—they are speaking to each other only "by sideways glances."

The eyes are the mirrors of the soul, as the saying goes … If we look down into their depths, we will see the heart.

Praying with the Gaze

Praying is speaking, yes, but especially gazing! It is normal that words should become fewer with time, everything has been said. What should then be done, if not pursue the encounter through a simple gaze? We know the Lord is watching us and we respond to his gaze. We are together. We are happy. Not with a joy that overflows into emotional feelings, but with a spiritual peace and happiness that spreads throughout our whole being.

Come to prayer, settle down, quiet and relaxed. Take a moment to recollect yourself in silence. Once you are calmed down, imagine Christ present in front of you at an exact place on the floor. Let yourself be simply gazed upon by him. Or peer into the depths of his face.

Do not strive to imagine many details about him: his height, his attitude, clothes of this or that color. Simply affirm through your faith that he is there, present, at an exact place on the floor and look at him "like one that opens his eyes with the advertence of love."[2] Use your imagination to serve your faith. Obviously, Jesus is not there, close by, in the precise way you imagine him to be, but he is there nonetheless and your imagination is only helping you to be aware of that.

To know you are gazed upon and to know you are loved! This method of prayer is the most effective one I know to experience the presence of Christ. We go to him without any obstacles or artificial devices. A real door open to the encounter with the Risen Christ. Fasten your gaze on his until your attention is totally centered on him and him alone. Remain at rest. Two or three seconds. As soon as another image or some alien thought tries to sneak in, gaze upon him again with great calm, just long enough to let the thought disappear.

We have seen previously how you can use a short formula at the beginning of prayer with a twofold objective:

breaking away from your former occupations and putting yourself in the presence of God. Here, the exchange of gazes performs the same work.

If the previous chapter was addressed to "listeners," this one is addressed more to "seers." Since this is the most dynamic part of your imagination, the one always risking being the first to be sidetracked, you must keep it busy. If it is the listening section, give it an expression "to chew on." If it is the visual one, provide an image.

The process is the same as for the invocation of which I have spoken: gaze at him every time your mind turns away from him and wanders about, then move from this gaze to the silence of his presence when you are seized by it. Keep all intruders away by gazing upon him again.

Looking at him. Letting him look at you. His gaze upon you, tender, comforting, full of mercy. Your gaze on him, full of trust and gratitude.

The warmer the gaze you cast on him, the more the ensuing silence will tend to prolong itself in total quietude. Or if in your case the gaze is in the other direction, that is from Christ to you, the more his gaze will be perceived as a loving one, the more you will be able to make it "resonate" in peace within you. As Charles de Foucauld wrote: "The best prayer is the one where there is the most love. It is all the better when the gazes of the soul are most filled with love, when the soul remains more tenderly and lovingly before its God."[3]

An extremely simple prayer: the loving attention of the heart visualizes the Lord and the whole being is turned to this presence. You do not meditate on him; you do not try to imagine him too much; only as needed for the heart to remain alert.

> I am not asking you now to think of him, or to form numerous conceptions of him, or to make long and subtle meditations with your understanding. I am asking you only to look at him. For who can prevent you from turning the eyes of your soul (just for a moment, if you can do no more) upon this Lord? […] Your Spouse never takes his eyes off you, daughters. […] He is only waiting for us to look at him, as he says to the Bride.[4]

Do not bother to imagine the details of his face or his clothes. That would only distract you. St. Teresa of Avila, whom I have just quoted and who often prayed in this way, said that she never managed to imagine Jesus' face. She only felt that he was near her, as you may have a perfect sense of the presence of a person whom you cannot see clearly in a dark room.

Gaze upon Christ without words, be uniquely busy in being amazed by him. Tell him you love him only through your gaze, your lips and even your thoughts being silent. The best prayer is the one where there is the greatest love.

A Gaze That Transforms

If necessary, use an icon of the Lord—one that is always painted in such a way that Christ seems to have his eyes fixed directly on the person looking at his picture.

Have you ever compared a statue of the Buddha with an icon illustrating a saint? The contrast could not be more significant. The Buddha is most often represented in the shape of a triangle, seated with his legs folded back, the hands (the active part) more or less still in the center of the triangle, plump, eyes closed, the face wearing the smile of one who has reached enlightenment. The saint of the icon is standing, emaciated by his self-denial; the garment, all in vertical lines, leads to owlish eyes, wide open, contemplating the Invisible. And, by gazing upon him, the viewer lets himself be transformed by him. "What we know is this: when he is revealed, we will be like him, for we will see him as he is" (*1 Jn* 3:2).

> Saying nothing, gazing upon you
> Asking for you with our eyes,
> Thanking you with our eyes.
> Closing our eyes because you are there,
> Opening them to see your smile.
> Becoming more and more your image
> From gazing upon you.[5]

During the eleventh century, the name "prayer of the simple gaze" was given to a certain precise degree of prayer. Gazing and contemplating, the two go together. If, for a few seconds, you succeed in remaining under his gaze in this way, say no more, do no more. Remain gently absorbed in his presence. The less you move, the better Our Lord does his work.

As soon as the mind starts to wander, gently place yourself again before him: "He is there, present." Go back to this as often as necessary. Fifty or sixty times, no matter.

> When your heart wanders or is distracted, bring it back gently to its center and set it again tenderly near to its Master. Should you do nothing else throughout your whole hour but take your heart and set it again close to Our Lord, and should you do so again as many times as it turns away from him, you will have used your hour very well.[6]

Stimulating, just the same! In passing, note the word "tenderly"…

Notes

[1] Christian de Chergé, quoted in Marie-Christine Ray, *Christian de Chergé, prieur de Tibhérine* (Paris: Bayard/Centurion, 1998), p. 72.

[2] *The Complete Works of Saint John of the Cross*, vol. 3, *Living Flame of Love*, p. 161.

[3] Charles de Foucauld, *Écrits spirituels*, 13th ed. (Paris: J. de Girord, 1957), p. 161.

[4] *The Complete Works of Saint Teresa of Jesus*, vol. 2, *Way of Perfection*, p. 107.

[5] Didier Rimaud, quoted in *Fêtes et saisons*, nº 326, June-July 1978, p. 17.

[6] St. Francis de Sales, *Œuvres*, critical edition of Annecy, vol. 18, p. 37.

5

… daring to make an affectionate gesture

"See with what mutual
embraces of affection
you must love
and embrace him in return,
he who has valued you
at such a great price."[1]
St. Bernard

Let us cast a glance at our two lovers. Two hands tenderly joined together on the white tablecloth …

Praying with a Gesture

As in the previous case, imagine the Lord present before you, but this time very close, within reach. And instead of only looking at him, express your love for him with a gesture of affection. No exterior movement: simply through visualization. In your imagination, express a movement of your heart for the Lord, with a small gesture, a physical attitude, posture. And put a little tenderness and warmth in this attitude, in this gesture. I warn you immediately that it is more compromising – a gesture is worth a thousand words – but what an extraordinary prayer!

Take an example. At a set moment, you go to your prayer corner and recollect yourself for a few seconds. Then, immediately, you imagine Christ on the cross right in front of you. (I deliberately use this picture because it is the most common one, but this is only a suggestion. During the Christmas season, the crib with the Child would serve just as well.) Imagine you are in Mary Magdalene's place for example. To begin your prayer, without making any physical movement, but within yourself, put your forehead on the lower part of the cross. Or embrace the blood-covered feet of the crucified One. Or, still more, put your arms around his feet, lean on his chest, bend over his open side. That is what Fr. Besnard encourages us to do:

> If [the Father] has given us his Son in flesh, it is so that we may embrace him fully with hands of flesh. […] Christ is there, open for you on the Cross, he will not fail you, He is nailed, it is up to you to run to him, to draw close to him, to embrace him. He lets others hold him: do not let him go before he has blessed you! This is his way of holding you in turn. He has made himself your prey, and this is his way of making you become his own.[2]

Once you have made the gesture, do no more, except letting yourself be moved by him. Be content to experience him within yourself by allowing him to resound in you. You have achieved the goal of your prayer: to remain in his presence.

That lasts for a few seconds. Then, unconsciously, you begin again to think of other things. As soon as you become aware of this, repeat your little gesture, always with some affection. If it is not neutral, if it is truly in agreement with what you feel for him, he will leave a small echo in your loving sensitivity. A few seconds at the most. Again a distraction … again repeat the gesture …

The approach is identical to that used for the prayer-word or for the prayer-gaze that we analyzed above. The aim is the same, concentrating your attention on the Beloved and arousing in yourself, if possible, a little stirring of love for him. The means is also the same, keeping your *mental* zone busy with a positively charged representation in order to arouse a discreet vibration in your *affective* zone, in such a way as to make your whole being attracted to him. The ultimate goal is the same: to remain, however little this may be, in this full silence, indwelt by him. Only the tool changes: a gesture, a caress, instead of a word or a gaze.

Note that you can join the one to the other. It would be wonderful if what you wish to express to God were conveyed both by a word and a gesture, the one completing the other, even penetrating each other. You repeat your formula while you make your gesture. You have two tools, an auditive and a visual one, to keep your *mental* zone focused on God, starting from two different angles. There will be so many fewer occasions to wander.

A Varied Range

If you are naturally effusive, extroverted, demonstrative with others, you will probably be the same in your prayer. Give yourself permission to be so. Grasp his feet with your hands, embrace the legs of the crucified Christ, hold his body tight, kiss his wounds. If you are not of Mediterranean blood, but more reserved by nature, simply remain more discreet, keep to more restrained gestures. Raise your hands up to him. Like the woman of the Gospel who was suffering from a hemorrhage (*Lk* 8:44), be satisfied to come up behind him and only touch the fringe of his clothes. If this is still too much, just sit at his feet like Mary of Bethany (*Lk* 10:39), sitting still, taking pleasure in being with him as long as you can.

> Imagine that the Lord himself is at your side and see how lovingly and how humbly he is teaching you – and, believe me, you should stay with so good a Friend for as long as you can before you leave him. If you become accustomed to having him at your side, and if he sees that you love him to be there and are always trying to please him, you will never be able, as we put it, to send him away, nor will he ever fail you. He will help you in all your trials and you will have him everywhere. Do you think it is a small thing to have such a Friend as that beside you? O sisters, those of you whose minds cannot reason for long or whose thoughts cannot dwell *upon God* but are *constantly* wandering must at all costs form this habit. I know quite well that you are capable of it.[3]

It is enough for you to feel comfortable with what you are doing. Let it be the real you expressing yourself. If the expression is authentic, the gesture you make will always be the right one. When we hug someone, we do not wonder for a week whether we are doing the right thing, whether it is the right gesture to make, whether it is done the right way, etc. We love the person and we hug him and that is all. Perhaps, in our interpersonal relationships we may commit blunders, but not here. God will always love us beyond all the testimony we can bring him. And our demonstrations of love, as bold as they may seem to us, will always fall short of what we should be doing and of what he is hoping from us. Our boldest attitude will always be only a heartless stammering.

There are active gestures and there are passive gestures. Those with which I love and those by which I let myself be loved. The masculine and feminine poles of our being, if you wish.

You *love* when you are the one resting on his shoulder, when you are the one putting your arms around him or embracing him. When you imagine him sitting in front of you and you are placing your hands in his. When you grasp his hands and kiss them. When you caress his face.

On the contrary, you *let yourself be loved* when you let him caress your hair to be comforted, when you let yourself be supported or uplifted by him. When you agree to be clasped on his chest by him.

Even if you are using some object to help you. If you wish to rest your forehead on the cross, do so on a pillar with your eyes closed. Lend your hands to God and bury your face in them. You feel driven to rest your head on his shoulder? Do so using the pew right in front of you. I know some that use a cushion or a pillow.

Repeat the gesture every time you need to. With your short formula if possible. Here again, the important thing is the loving silence. The type of gesture has no importance. Use the one that comes to you, but perform it putting in it all your affectionate leanings. You do not come to reflect but to love.

The trick is to experience this gesture as intensely and as tenderly as possible. A minimum of imagination and a maximum of affection. To love and to let yourself be loved, to embrace and to let yourself be caressed.

You will ultimately become something of the adulteress who spent a whole meal at Jesus' feet, kissing the latter, washing them with her tears and wiping them with her hair.

> The soul lies down at his feet, bathing them with her tears, anointing them. [...] She imagines all that in a strongly physical way which, because of the very sweetness of this sensitive imagination, often earns for her certain flashes of enlightenment and a warm desire for spiritual prayer and contemplation. Without knowing how, these physical images make her understand certain mysteries of devotion.[4]

Or be somewhat like John at the Last Supper, his head leaning on Jesus' chest. An hour of prayer you will remember.

On one of the portals of the cathedral of Chartres, a medieval sculptor pictured the cycle of creation according to the account in Genesis. We see, in successive tableaux, God creating the heavenly bodies, then the birds and so on. Finally comes the scene where he is shaping Adam. The Creator is seated, leaning a little forward over his work and Adam, still inert, has his head resting on God's lap. The latter, with his two caressing and artistic hands, is tracing the features of Adam's face in the clay that is still damp. He is shaping his hair with a few light strokes, molding his cheeks with a smiling cajolery. Adam is letting himself be pampered, motionless and asleep, still shapeless from the waist down, his legs disappearing into the clay from which he is made.

Ah! If only we could become like this Adam, totally at peace in these creating hands, just for the period of prayer!

Letting ourselves be drawn from the clay, built up and sculpted by those hands. Without any other concern except to let them do their work. Letting ourselves be modeled so that they may shape us as they please. Praying while we let God create us, caress and remake us. Spend a half-hour in this attitude and you will tell me that it is too short.

Suppose now that you gradually discover that your "overall attitude" before God consists in finding a refuge in the Lord. You have experienced, quite regularly, in and outside your prayer, the feeling of being poor and fragile, of being somewhat fearful in the face of the future. So you seek to be sustained and supported by God. And, the other day, you caught yourself by surprise – it came all by itself – you were humming to him: "Keep me, O Lord my God, You my only hope." You do not remember too well where it comes from,[5] but it has become your formula. It expresses you so well. The only drawback is that it is a bit long. So you have broken it down into three parts, one breath for each: "Keep me / O Lord my God / You my only hope."

Could you not express the same experience with an image, while you are at it? To help you, this time use a painting. The one of the *Return of the Prodigal Son* by Rembrandt is quite well known; it does not need to be described here.

At the beginning of your prayer, put yourself, like the son in the painting, down on your knees, leaning on the Father, coiled up in his cloak. Always in the line of your own prayer, that of handing yourself over into the hands of a God who sustains and protects. While humming your little refrain.

Now, *you* are the one who, in your own insecurity, are clinging onto him. You then take notice of the fact that it is *your* head that is resting on his chest. An active love.

Now, *he* is the one leaning over you and wrapping you in his cloak. This time you take notice of the fact that *his* very hands are warming your shoulders. Let yourself be loved. A passive love.

The same image, the same gesture of love, the same experience basically, but with variations. On Monday evening, the whole day having been trying, you are the one hiding close to him during prayer time. Tuesday, a calmer day, you will have less need of being comforted then, so he is rather the one calling you, welcoming you and clasping you on his heart. Wednesday, something else, still a different tone for your prayer … It will take you years to exhaust the meaning of this one painting by Rembrandt.

I have been using the same gesture for a long time. As for my short formula, I say to myself that I should change from time to time, but … the same one always comes back. And still, it is never exactly the same one. Is not love always new, even if it always uses the same vocabulary and the same gestures? When I explain this way of praying to a group, someone often comes to me after the lecture to tell me stealthily:

"I was already praying like that, but I never dared to speak about it for fear of being declared mental."

"Rest assured, you are normal. Love, whatever it may be, even for God, always ends up being expressed in this way, grudgingly if necessary. Love is creative. Basically, everything is allowed to the one who loves."

There is often another listener wearing an increasingly quizzical look on his face as the lecture unfolds. Exasperated, he ends up by letting out his comment:

"Come on … We don't do things like that with God …!"

A Privilege, Thanks to the Incarnation

"Why yes, precisely we do."

And that is thanks to the incarnation. You would be right if God had not made himself man. Being man in Jesus, God becomes accessible: he has a body, a face, a voice and a language similar to ours. In Jesus Christ, this road is a two-way route: that of God coming to us and that of us going to God.

As Christians, we believe that God, the Transcendent One, the All-Other, the Unknowable, made himself known in a man's body, that of Christ, in whom dwells "the whole fullness of deity" (*Col* 2:9). He is "the image of the invisible God" (*Col* 1:15). "The Word became flesh and lived among us, and we have seen his glory" (*Jn* 1:14). So he chose that route to come to us. And we also believe that we may go to God by using the same route, that is, Our Lord's humanity. Does not Christ say that he is the Way and that no one goes to the Father except through him (cf. *Jn* 14:6). "Whoever has seen me has seen the Father" (*Jn* 14:7).

Of course, the Jews, for example, or the Moslems cannot, in the strict sense, pray exactly as we do: allowing to God the possibility of using body language to communicate himself. To be sure, they speak of God as having "eyes that see" and "hands that act with mightiness." But they are not fooled by their own words: they well know that these are anthropomorphisms, "ways of speaking." The Old Testament also says that God has "wings"[6] to shelter us ... Their refusal to represent God with images made with human hands is more than significant for their theology on this point: God is beyond all knowledge and all visibility and therefore cannot be represented in an image.

Christians have adopted a totally different attitude: the Invisible has taken a body and a face. He was seen, heard and touched. He died, then rose from the dead in his flesh. He was, is forever both true God and true man at the same time.

But accepting the incarnation is difficult! I have just demonstrated that in relation to prayer. To dare to touch God ... That is not done! Sacrilege!

We could do the same by examining the history of the Church. Take the famous iconoclastic quarrel[7] in the Eastern Church. The icon is a testimony given to the incarnation. We should be able to represent God since he has chosen to make himself visible, and, for the same reason, we should logically be able to render homage to him through the icon. It is a matter of making the distinction between the *veneration* given to the image and the *adoration* given to God alone. But how many combats had to be waged to arrive at this!

It is hardly any better in the Western World. Teresa of Avila tells us that, under God's guidance, she had reached a high degree of contemplation by centering her attention on the passion of the Lord. We must remember that she belonged to the same century as the Spanish realist artists who excelled in the representations of the scourged and crucified Christ. She came across "some books written about prayer" which "advise us earnestly to put aside all corporeal imagination and to approach the contemplation of the Divinity," for "anything else … will hinder or impede those who have arrived so far from attaining to the most perfect contemplation." "As this work [contemplation] is entirely spiritual, anything corporeal (even Christ's humanity) may disturb or impede it." She who loved so much to keep company with Jesus at Gethsemane … Here, she was being advised against this.

At first, she followed these instructions. She was going astray… Then doubt awakened in her mind. To be sure, she admitted that "God leads souls along many roads and by many ways." She nonetheless concluded, "I believe it to be mistaken." She thought it was a great grace when "the Lord allows her to stand with Saint John, at the foot of the Cross." "Not to endeavour with all our strength to have always before us … this most sacred Humanity," "the soul is left … in the air." "We are not angels and we have bodies." "As a rule, our thoughts must have something to lean upon."

"We have a very good Friend in Christ. We look at him as a Man […] and he becomes our Companion. Once we have made a habit of thinking of him in this way, it becomes very easy to find him at our side." Finally, she concluded, "Do not seek another road even if you are at the summit of contemplation."[8]

It is not only the incarnation of the Word lost in a haze, it is also our own corporeal condition. Contemporary anthropological thought teaches us that not only do we "have a body," but that, more precisely, we "are a body." And psychology goes further by demonstrating that up to 60% of our language is non-verbal. Therefore it is body language.

From that we may presume that the body would also hold a significant place in our spiritual adventure. The human being, at least for the time being, does not exist outside of or beside its body. We need it to express everything we live in our most intimate selves. In the first place our loves. From that we may then deduce that we need our body just as much as our spiritual faculties to activate our interior lives. The way to promote this interior life, whatever its nature, necessarily involves the body.

It seems that we tend to do away with this reality as soon as we set about praying. Indeed, being pure spirits would be so much simpler, to be rid of this cumbersome body. The proof? Go and see any spiritual director (as we used to say), tell him that you no longer can pray as you should and ask him for advice. He will invariably answer something like this: "Concentrate more" or "Think only of God and reject all the rest." I translate this: "Prayer is performed between the eyes and the hat." But no. Love concerns the whole being. Soul and body. Perhaps the body especially.

We must learn to take prayer out of our heads. At first, it always works, but after some time, the head is no longer a very good place to pray. Broaden and deepen your prayer by leaving the area of reasoning. Remember: "Do not think so much but love much."

Obviously, praying in this way has its drawbacks. Do not be surprised if the words, images and gestures that you use refer to affectionate experiences that you have already had in other circumstances. For better or for worse. This is due to the fact that each one of us possesses a certain personal "vocabulary," coined throughout our affective life. It is with this totally personal range, necessarily limited, often going back to our childhood, that we express our emotions, our ties and our rejections. Praying being very simply one of the forms of expression of love, we cannot do other than use this vocabulary that is proper to us.

If, during your childhood, you had a perturbed relationship with your father, Rembrandt's painting will not be the best representation to use to express your relationship with God. No panic, very simply choose another one.

If you are married, at one time or another, words and gestures that you use with your partner will very likely emerge in this form of prayer. The opposite would be surprising. To become aware of this will help you to use them judiciously.[9]

Where Is Your God?

One last point. When, for a moment, you happen to have the feeling of the presence of God, where is this presence sensed? I know very well that God is present everywhere. My question simply refers to the subjective perception you have of it. God's manifestation (felt subjectively) addressed to you, makes you "turn to him." In what direction? Such is my question.

Most of the examples I have given until now (leaning your forehead on the cross, embracing the legs of the Crucified One, sitting at his feet, leaning on his chest, placing your hands in his open hands, etc.) suppose that God is on an equal *face-to-face* with you. Each time he is placed before or right beside you. Let us say that most of the time, it is God the Son.

In Christian prayer, the Son *reveals* the Father, the Son whom we look at, listen to and touch so that he may unveil him for us (cf. *Jn* 1:18). "We have touched the Word of life with our hands, this life was revealed" (*1 Jn* 1-2). He is the *Good Shepherd* (cf. *Jn* 10:11) who takes us by the hand and guides us. He is the *Vine* (*Jn* 15:5) on which we must remain, to which we must cling. He is the *Friend* (*Jn* 15:15) in whom we confide, on whom we lean in every sense of the word. His name means "Savior" (cf. *Mt* 1:21): we may take shelter under his cloak. He is the *Big Brother* (*Heb* 2:10-17) whose hand we must hold to go through our trials.

I showed my preference for this type of images because they are the ones I use personally, and so it is easier for me to speak about them. But, for all that, I do not intend to impose them *urbe et orbi* … It may be that when you encounter God, he is not seen spontaneously so much as someone on an equal face-to-face with you, but one who *encompasses* you. Like someone enwrapping you, surrounding and supporting you. That varies according to the impulses of the Spirit and the psychological tendencies proper to each one. So all things being considered, this is more about God the Father.

He is the one who "gives to all mortals life and breath and all things" (*Acts* 17:25). We come to draw from him. We take refuge in his arms …

If this is your case, your task will consist in finding corresponding images to sustain your prayer with an action language that suits you. Finding your own "vocabulary." I remember a poster illustrating, in a close-up, a small child calmly resting in the palm of an open hand. Feel yourself being borne in this way by the hand of God, why not? Visualize yourself in this way in prayer …

One of my friends' professors, of a certain age, sometimes catches himself sitting on the knees of the Heavenly Father, rocking with him. As a child, he knew his parents loved him. But since they were fourteen seated around the table and the father had much to do to provide food for all his family, he had little free time to show his care for each one of his children, one at a time. Not to mention the day's weariness. And add to that the male reserve. But when he came home in the evening and sat in his rocking chair to read the paper, the child would climb on his knees between him and the paper. He was rarely spoken to, he was often hugged, always had an approving smile. These sweet moments remained etched in his memory. They are part of a "vocabulary" he received and uses, almost without wishing to, for his prayer. My friend snuggles against the Father and lets the latter rock him.

But perhaps in your case, God is perceived neither as an equal nor as one encompassing you, but as someone *inside* you. An intimate presence in your heart, sometimes even a physical warmth within yourself. This time, the Spirit, the one dwelling in us. In this case as well, appropriate attitudes will have to be found.

There was a Russian staretz who taught his disciples to keep in prayer their minds and their thoughts fixed on objects set uniquely within the boundaries of their bodies, to think of nothing outside the limits of their skin. When applied methodically, this advice would help the novices gradually to live within themselves, precisely where the Spirit of God dwells.

Leaning onto Christ, curling up in the Father's hands, entering within oneself to reach the Spirit. Starting this over again ten, twenty, fifty times if need be. In his mercy, God will not leave you all by yourself …

Notes

[1] St. Bernard, *Deuxième sermon après l'octave de l'Épiphanie*, quoted in Sister Agnès Lemaire, *Saint Bernard et le mystère du Christ* (Quebec: Anne Sigier, 1991), p. 43.

[2] A.-M. Besnard, O.P., *Propos intempestifs sur la prière* (Paris: Cerf, 1978), pp. 85-86.

[3] *The Complete Works of Saint Teresa of Jesus*, vol. 2, *Way of Perfection*, p. 106.

[4] William of St. Thierry, *Exposé sur le Cantique des Cantiques*, trans. M. Dumontier (Paris: Cerf, 1962), p. 91.

[5] It is an antiphon of one of the responsorial psalms of the Paschal Vigil. Adapted from Psalm 16:1.

[6] *Ps* 17:8; 36:7; 57:1; 61:4, 63:7, etc.

[7] The word means "destroyer of images." For more than a century (726-843), the iconoclastic crisis raised successive waves of violence and persecutions within the Byzantine Church. Arising from the popular devotion to icons, it presented two contradictory theological conceptions about the images of Christ. According to the first, these images were necessarily heretical since, of a material nature, they separated or confused the two natures, human and divine, of the Savior. According to the other conception, of which John Damascene was the great theologian, icons are visible signs of the sanctification of matter made possible by the incarnation of Christ. The Council of Nicaea II condemned iconoclasm as a heresy.

[8] *The Complete Works of Saint Teresa of Jesus*, vol. 1, *Life*, chapter 22, pp. 136 ff. *passim*.

[9] Here the question of the eventual eruptions of eroticism in this process comes up. I think that when one becomes aware of this, prayer must be stopped immediately (since there is a deviation and that is not the aim).

That person must move on to other occupations and go back to prayer the next day and go easy with it.

To my knowledge, this is a rare phenomenon among men, but more likely to happen with women because *(1)* the Jesus sought in prayer is a male, *(2)* sexuality being more diffused in women than in men and more difficult to separate from simple tenderness, it is easier to slip from the latter to the former.

The worst mistake would be to deny the fact systematically. To acknowledge, without dwelling on it, that the pleasures of the body are an aspect of the experience of lofty mysticism is a sign of spiritual wholeness. A sexuality that is repressed because of its incompatibility with the experience of God has every chance of surging up elsewhere and, this time, in a pathological form. On this subject, see Antoine Vergote, *Dette et désir. Deux axes chrétiens et la dérive pathologique* (Paris: Seuil, 1978), pp. 165-304.

6
… walking arm in arm

"For the one
who prays constantly,
the entire world
becomes church."
Staretz Silouan

One of the current pitfalls of spiritual life is to lose the presence of God at our side or in ourselves. This presence then becomes an abstract notion, the object of our thoughts and meditations. It has no longer anything to do with our behavior.

Making the Presence of God Real

If you are caught in this trap, I suggest to you a means of freeing yourself. One fine evening, instead of being glued to the television set, go out for a healthy walk. Go at least as far as the shopping center. Not all by yourself: with the Beloved. As soon as you have walked past the door, take the Lord's arm and, especially, do not let him go! Walk slowly with him. Tell him what you have in your heart that you would like to tell him: your day, your desire for him, your joy in being with him for a short while.

Let it be said in passing that if you meet anyone, do not be concerned about what he might think: half of the passers-by talk to themselves in the street. But as for you, you know that you are not alone …

Perhaps you have nothing to tell him. This is still better. So, be quiet. Do nothing but be with him and walk by his side. All your heart leaning towards him. Your whole attention centered on him. All your love directed to him, attentive to him.

> Upon my bed at night,
> I seek him whom my soul loves;
> I seek him, but find him not;
> I must rise now and go about the city,
> in the streets and in the squares;
> I must seek him whom my soul loves.
> I seek him, but find him not.
> The sentinels find me,
> as they go about in the city.
> "Have you seen him whom my soul loves?"
> Scarcely have I passed them,
> when I find him whom my soul loves.
> *I hold him, and will not let him go.*[1]

During the half-hour walk, time for the round trip to the shopping center (or time for the television soap opera, if you prefer), be all his, only with him. Place your head on his shoulder, rest on him, partly close your eyes (not too much so you can see the lampposts), clasp him against yourself.

> If I met you outside, I would kiss you,
> and no one would despise me.
> I would lead you and bring you

into the house of my mother.
You would initiate me;
I would give you spiced wine to drink,
the juice of my pomegranates.
O that his left hand were under my head,
and that his right hand embraced me![2]

The important thing is to make it real. This is not an initiative of the mind, or even, strictly speaking, of the imagination. This is an initiative of the whole person who wants to be with someone who is loved. Make this real until your *affective* zone is working.

It is easier to do than it seems. Easier than when you are in a chapel, for you are freer in your movements, less frozen by the décor. You are less afraid of being judged daft if a sigh or a gesture escapes you.

There, I dare you to do this for half an hour, two or three times a week, without Christ catching up to you in front of the grocery store. Start as early as this evening. Tell your spouse that you are going for a walk arm in arm with your lover. The worst that can happen to you is that she will hire a private detective to watch you.

A certain lady, brought up in the Orthodox faith but not too fervent, experienced a conversion when she became a widow. And this conversion had this peculiar aspect: it consisted in discovering that Christ was constantly by her side. So, since she was living alone, she gradually developed the habit of speaking to Jesus in a familiar tone, while doing her housecleaning, while making her meals. She made comments to him about her encounters, her concerns and her joys. In short, whereas everyone thought she was alone in her house, in fact, there were two.

But one fine day, she came out more preoccupied than she usually was by her grocery list, and it was only once she was on the sidewalk that she gave a start, her hand on her mouth and eyes wide open:

"Oh! I forgot to bring Jesus!"

What a mistake! She went back, opened the door, entered half-way in the doorframe:

"So, Jesus, you are coming?"

They left again … both of them this time. At least we may suppose they did.

This is a caricature. We could scoff at her naïveté. But she had no problems in her life of prayer. In this sense, she could teach us something, even if we have just caught her in the act of "having a distraction." Compared to her, I must admit that, in my case, my whole daily life is an almost continuous distraction and that I am rarely caught by surprise in the act "of being in prayer." And still more rarely "of being with Jesus" to the same degree she was.

Here are other examples, just for the sake of variety. You are in your car, alone. A trip you make every day and that you know by heart. Such a routine that at a red light, always the same, you recognize other drivers, always the same ones, making the same trip you are, at the same time of day as you.

Make of this trip by yourself an outing for two with your Beloved. Place him beside you … and sing a hymn or a liturgical motet to him. Choose something that moves you, that awakens something in you making you really feel like singing to him. We all have our favorites.

I say a hymn, but why not a simple song of worldly love that you transpose into the mystical world?

> What would I be without you,
> who are coming to meet me …?[3]
>
> I would like to tell you how much I love you
> But not with the words of everyday
>
> I would like to write a poem for you
> that would be more beautiful than love.[4]

Why not? The fact of singing, the song itself through its rhythm and melody, easily stir feelings and emotions. So why not use them as a channel towards the One you want as your Lover? Our Christian education has trained us to stifle rather than use our affective impulses … Make use of your usual movements to create a similar companionship. I will always remember my journeys as a student on the subway, before I entered the monastery. The trip was a rather long one, always the same, morning and night; I knew it by heart. I used these trips to travel with someone else. I think that, since then, I have never found such formidable opportunities again, even here at the monastery. Nor have I found a more effective recipe for prayer.

A Daily Routine with Him

These "true" encounters do not have to be made outside the house or outside the usual schedule.

Place a small icon on your bedside table. At night, as you lie down glance at it for a moment, commend yourself into his hands. Not only in thought but again in a real way. Make your bed, into which you are slipping for the night, the two joined hands of God in the palms of which you fall asleep. Let your blankets be his hands that tuck you in bed.

During a period of insomnia, rest your head on the pillow as on his shoulder. Close your eyes to snuggle well up to him. The pillow may become for you the Beloved on whom you try to lean.

You are running your errands? You are passing a drugstore? In the sun warming your face and body, see the love of the Father setting you aflame with his warmth. The wind is blowing and caressing your face? See there the Spirit surrounding you, driving you on, shaking off the old dust.

You are bringing your accounts up to date? You are preparing the meal? Let him have a small space by your side. Ask him to keep you company.

I am giving you some leads, it is up to each one of you to find the places and the means for the Lord to become a true presence, I was going to say, a concrete and palpable presence.

Even in monastic life, work may become absorbing. And if the monk does not manage to live and especially to work in the presence of God, he is done for. As the one responsible for the orchard of the community, I learned, to my great disillusion, that the insect pests are the same here as at the neighbors', having no regard for our style of life, and the market restrictions are the same for everyone.

So I am constantly torn between two demands. On the one hand, prayer takes up some of my time and prevents me from doing the work that is my task at the monastery. On the other hand, work is constantly gnawing at the time I would like to devote to prayer, for which I became a monk.

There is only one solution: *pray while you work*. Which does not mean saying your rosary nonstop. This is not passive. I would end up crashing into an apple tree with the tractor. This would kill my urge to recite Aves for the rest of my days. It is a matter of working arm in arm with him. We would need two persons in the tractor cabin: myself, the visible one, and he, the invisible one.

You have surely already seen a photo of a dining room in a monastery. As you may notice, the monks eat seated on one side of the table only, the space in front of each of them remains empty. I was molded, as a novice, in this way of doing things without asking myself any questions up to the day when I had the opportunity of spending some time in a monastery that had given up this custom. I had my meals with the community, that is, with a good monk of a very sympathetic nature, sitting across from me. I must say that we had our meals in silence. But how this holy man annoyed me! He had no business being there! He was more than a meter away from me, but I had the impression that he was picking in my plate. Try hard as I did, there was no way of carrying on as if he were not there!

I blamed my uneasiness on my reflexes proper to "a crusty old boy." Until I became aware that, effectively, he was taking someone else's place. He was rather in Someone's place. Without being conscious of this, I had adopted this ancient tradition of having my meal *with him*. "If you hear my voice and open the door, I will come in to you and eat with you, and you with me" (*Rev* 3:20).

We may say prayers without praying. It happens to me … We may also pray without saying any prayers. I would like this to happen to me more often.

Transform Your Short Breaks into Small Deserts

Too often we try to make *whole hours* available for prayer. But it rarely happens that we have one of these hours where, first, we have nothing to do, and when, secondly, we feel like praying. Most of the time, either we have a spare hour but we do not feel like praying, or we feel like praying but the hour we would need is not available.

On the other hand, each of our days is broken into small deserts, that is, into short intervals between two occupations that *could* become moments of immersion into the presence of God. Short moments which, most of the time, we idle away, but where we could learn to gaze at him. Short breaks that we can either use or waste.

Raise your eyes up to him while your meal is in the microwave oven; while you are waiting for the telephone to be free, while you are waiting for the bus, while you are going up or down in the elevator.

Modern life, in spite of all, leaves us with a series of small opportunities to give a little wink to the Lord, just in passing. But we let them go by. We are somewhat like the heron in Lafontaine's fable that was searching for food along a stream. In the morning, he refused a noble carp, for his appetite was not yet keen enough. Later in the day, he did not find any fish which, even more common, would have been worthy of him. In the evening, he would have liked to find some small fry, but he had to be satisfied with an insignificant slug.

We wait until we have a complete hour available. God has planned short moments for us, like small sandwiches, there on the corner of the desk, but we wait for an official invitation to the restaurant for a meal with an appetizer, hors-d'œuvre, main dish and dessert. A whole hour with nothing on the menu except to meet him. But there is the risk that this hour will not be given to us, and we will end our day without having prayed.

Note the tiny spaces available, identify in advance the most favorable moments. Create them if you have to. "The one who does not have a half-hour perhaps has three times ten minutes or even ten times three minutes."[5] Will the task that is so urgent be totally jeopardized if you take two minutes of internalization before you begin? Will cutting off five minutes from your sleep, morning or evening, harm your health seriously? Could the broom or the computer wait for a short time without the sky falling on your head?

Madeleine Delbrêl,[6] who was a heavy smoker, had the habit of lighting up a cigarette in silence and taking a puff before engaging herself in a conversation. When one of her lady colleagues questioned her about this "little mania," she replied:

"This gives me a few seconds to put God in the picture."

Once you have found (or created) a little desert, how should you best use it? "Myself, built as I am, what takes me faster to God …? In thirty seconds?" Looking at the landscape through the window? Going back to the prayer-word, the prayer-gesture? A more elaborate prayer like the *Our Father?* Think of the Angelus of the past … Gazing at a crucifix?

Or simply kneeling down, without saying anything? Prayer of the body is something beautiful. Be still for a moment. Stop running in order to recollect yourself.

Of course, this is not easy. You must work to find these little deserts, they are not given. You must do some violence to habits, break down instances of sloth.

Moreover, do not be surprised if all sorts of enemies oppose this. Since biblical times, we have known that demons dwell in the desert. If you try to create little deserts, you may also expect little demons to emerge. For example, "Impatience": when you have to wait, stamping your feet comes more spontaneously than prayer. Or the demon "Day dreaming": when the mind is not busy, it travels. "Weariness" also: too tired to take hold of yourself. Especially the contemporary hordes of "stop-gap" demons that are legion and known by their singing like the sirens of Greek mythology. One of them is called "TV," another "Radio," still others "Walkman" and "Background Music." You are probably familiar with these. There is even one who sneaks into the telephone while you are waiting on the line; that one is called "Sentimental Music." They are the accomplices of a society that is afraid of silence. Your fear of interior life.

You will have to agree to struggle against them. To give preference to God will always imply some wearying, unexciting daily struggles and often … without great success.

Concrete Signs of His Presence

We have forgotten how to use visible signs that remind us of his presence, under the pretext of our faith being that of an "adult." Looking at a picture. Venerating an icon with a kiss. Putting a rose at the foot of a statue of the

Madonna. We use the excuse for our failure: "That is for children. That is for the poor." We forget that we are all paupers in prayer. That we should all become like little children (*Mt* 18:4). All the great saints kissed the crucifix. Sometimes this was the only thing they could still do when they were lying on their deathbed.

I was told about the trial of a monk who had experienced a terrible night of the faith. Unable to live the liturgy. Unable to pray by himself. Unable to do the slightest profitable reading. The only thing he could do during the three or four hours explicitly set aside every day for monastic prayer was to gaze at an icon of the Blessed Virgin. He would sit in a corner, place the icon on his knees and look at it. He did that and only that for hours until the Mother of God gradually led him back to her Son.

There are some seriously ill patients who are in a similar state. Unable to do any meditation: they fall asleep. Unable to read: their eyes are too worn out. All they can do is resort to very simple prayers, sustained by visible signs. A small plaque on which they find the fourteen stations of the Way of the Cross, for example. Just what is needed to make what I call "a minimal way of the cross" since they are unable to follow it around at all the stations for lack of stronger legs.

— First station: Jesus is arrested … For me … Jesus I love you.

And kiss the station. That is the most important. Then go on to the second one.

> "A priest went to visit a patient in his home. He noticed an empty chair at the patient's bedside and asked what it was doing there. The patient said, 'I had placed Jesus on that

chair and was talking to him before you arrived … For years I found it extremely difficult to pray until a friend explained to me that prayer was a matter of talking to Jesus. He told me to place an empty chair nearby, to imagine Jesus sitting on that chair and to speak to him and listen to what he says to me in reply. I have had no difficulty in praying ever since.' Some days later, so the story goes, the daughter of the patient came to the rectory to inform the priest that her father had died. She said, 'I left him alone for a couple of hours. He seemed so peaceful. When I got back to the room I found him dead. I noticed a strange thing, though: his head was not resting on the bed but on a chair that was beside his bed.'"[7]

This is the difference between "thinking of surrender" and "making the act of surrender." Imagine that Jesus is there beside you during your daily tasks. Speak to him often. Act as if he were there where you imagine him to be. Look at him, lean on him. This is an excellent way of having an intense experience of the living presence of the Risen One.

You will tell me, "This is too human." But, after all, what did God come to save? With whom did he make a covenant? Whom did he call to meet him? Brains walking around on legs? Disincarnated gray matter?

Did he not come rather for totally human beings, having a heart, a soul, reason, senses … There is a vast difference between a *brain* that is *thinking* of an *attribute of God* and a *whole human being meeting* a *real God*. Prayer is not a brain concentrating on one idea. It is my whole being entering into a relationship with a real and living God who loves me and whom I love. And not only someone of whom "I think." Not only do I think of him, but I live with him, beside him, immersed in him and indwelt by him.

Notes

[1] *Song* 3:1-4. Italics are added.

[2] *Song* 8:1-3. Italics are added.

[3] Louis Aragon, set to music by Jean Ferrat.

[4] Lyrics and music by Georges Dor.

[5] Jean-Marie Perrin, *Vivre avec Dieu* (Paris: Aubin, 1957), p. 52.

[6] Madeleine Delbrêl (1904-1964) converted from atheism at the age of 29 and committed herself to be a social worker in the working class suburbs of Paris. Contemplative and active at the same time, she lived by a radiant faith.

[7] Anthony de Mello, S.J., *Sadhana: A Way to God* (St. Louis: The Institute of Jesuit Sources, 1978), pp. 71-72.

7

… ever striving to love better

"Love that does not wish
to be total,
love that does not suffer
from being still imperfect,
is not love."[1]
Yves de Montcheuil

When we are in love and wish to know if our love is shared, we pluck off the petals of a daisy: … loves me, … loves me not, … a little, … much, … not at all, … passionately. This is not a very scientific method, but for lack of better … After all, if it does not tell me much about the other's feeling, it is at least a good indication of mine: something new is preoccupying me. Someone is dwelling in me enough for me to take time to play with a flower. A good sign.

We do not pluck the petals of daisies when we pray. Still, we ought to. I agree that this would not be a very scientific method to know if God loves us. But we do not have to guess that, we already know that he does. Or rather, he told us through his Son in the Gospel. Therefore, it is a fact that he loves us. But as for us, do we love him? Once the question has been asked, to be caught with a daisy in front of the tabernacle would be an excellent indication of a positive answer. So, I pray, … do not pray, … pray poorly, … little, … not at all, … passionately?

To answer this, we must once more go by way of the experience of love. Let us make a digression.

The Three Components of Love[2]

Every love experience implies three components. First of all, there is the *pleasure*. It is made up of what belongs to physical attraction, eroticism and sensuality in the broadest sense of the word. This includes a whole range, from the warm handshake to the sexual relationship.

Then there is *affection.* We understand by that everything in the order of sympathy, mutual esteem, warmth, tenderness, kindliness, etc. This means feeling good with someone, having the impression that we are accepted and able to share with that someone without feeling that we are being judged.

Finally, the *choice*, which introduces values, ethics. This requires some discernment in the experience, sometimes contradictory, and puts the chosen option to work. For example, eroticism, an aspect of *pleasure*, can pull the person in this or that direction, but if this person wants to grow in maturity and love as an adult, his *choice* will have to direct his behavior, keeping him away from certain ways of acting and favoring other ways.[3]

PLEASURE: "I find that being with you is most pleasant."

AFFECTION: "I can share my experience and my feelings with you."

CHOICE: "I am committing myself to you because of certain values I have."

In order for *love to be true*, the *three components must be present.* If one or more is missing, this love will not be a total one.

Take the case of a client-prostitute relationship. The client limits the relationship uniquely to the level of the *pleasure* component. There is no bond of *affection* with this woman who is there only for the time being. Neither does he make a *choice* since any woman would suit the purpose. This relationship, therefore, is not a love relationship since it lacks the three necessary components.

PLEASURE: "This is the only thing I seek."

AFFECTION (absent): "I do not want to be tied down to you."

CHOICE (absent): "You or another woman, no matter."

Another possible situation is that of a person unable to communicate his or her inner world to others, to share, to exchange. Here the blockage is on the level of the *affection* component. The classic example is that of a man spending an evening with his buddies, playing cards for hours with them, a glass of beer in hand that helps him to talk, and who ultimately confides to them, with the help of his tipsiness:

"Boys, you cannot know how much I love you …"

And adding with a blur in his voice:

"The problem is that I absolutely cannot say the same thing to my wife. Yet, I love her so very much …"

PLEASURE: "I feel attracted to you and we feel good when we are together."

AFFECTION (problematic): "I am unable to express the tender love I feel for you."

CHOICE: "I am committing myself to you because of certain values that I have."

The presence of the three components is always necessary for the love experience to be complete. But if we want to change the picture slightly, we must add that, according to the type of experience, one of the three components will dominate over the other two. In other words, one will be experienced with capital letters whereas the other two will only be in lower case. And that is according to the type of love relationship in which the person is engaged.

So in a "love at first sight" adventure, the intensity will be on the side of *pleasure*.

PLEASURE: **"I think it is wonderful to have met you and be able to be close to you."**

AFFECTION: "I really do not know you well yet because I have not shared in depth with you."

CHOICE: "I really did not decide to form this relationship; it imposed itself on me, as it were."

A shrewd individual said that in love, it is the beginnings that are delightful, and that is why we always start over again. He was not wrong because, with time, the relationship will have to be deepened and the other two components will have to be integrated into the experience to arrive at a total love. This requires a sustained effort. Since this is an arduous task, people prefer to start over again with another partner, with the most pleasant part, of course.

This is true even for prayer. Prayer is pleasant during the first week following the conversion. Much less so during the next fifty years.

In a friendship relationship, the *affection* dimension will dominate: sharing, being together, mutual understanding.

PLEASURE: "Your presence pleases me but is not indispensable."

AFFECTION: **"Our exchanges make me grow; our sharing helps me to live.**

CHOICE: "I agree to invest in our relationship."

To the astonishment of many no doubt, I add that the marital relationship must be classed in the present category: built on affection. That is why, in marital therapies of all kinds, the spouses are made to work on improving their communication skills in order to share what they experience on the emotional level. "Learn to express what you feel. Express what you experience inside. Contrary to what you think, your partner cannot guess that."[4] Not bad advice for prayer. Even if God can guess.

In friendship, *pleasure* is not totally absent: there is a certain warmth in handshakes, contacts and pats on the back. Similarly, *choice* is also present: we do not befriend just anybody.

Unless we are adolescents: this is the age of friendship *par excellence*, but sometimes at this time we have friends that have little to recommend them. The *pleasure* and *affection* dimensions take on totally new proportions, unknown until then, while, on the other hand, the capacity for making *choices* has not yet reached maturity. That is what makes parents tear out their hair at certain times.

It is still this same capacity to make ethical *choices* that intervenes when a friendly relationship with a person of the opposite sex becomes disturbing. In this relationship where *affection*, in the sense of interpersonal sharing, is dominant and *pleasure* is beginning to be too important, *choice* will have to intervene to clarify the situation. "Either I commit myself in a new type of relationship with this friend; or I reverse the engines in order not to make a mess of my life and that of the other."

In a relationship of charity, the *choice* dimension will come first.

PLEASURE: "I hope our contacts will be pleasant."

AFFECTION: "It would be desirable to be able to confide in each other."

CHOICE: **"I am committing myself to you for the sake of my values."**

Suppose for the sake of simplification, that these values are those of the Gospel. It is in their name, for example, that we live in a religious community. That we work with the poorest. That we become involved in catechetics. That we serve "meals on wheels" or that we take time to pray. But, here again, if the *choice* is the dominant factor, it would be preferable that solid *affective* relationships be established with the people for whom and with whom we commit ourselves as believers. And that we even *enjoy* working together. The love of charity would then be complete.

A Prayer in the Principal Register

Prayer is also an experience of love. In order for it to be wholesome, the three components of love are necessary.

But as we have seen already, one of the three will be dominant without, for all that, excluding the other two, and here it will be *affection*. Prayer is thus a friendship love with God.

PLEASURE: "I feel good in your presence."

AFFECTION: "You know me down to my innermost depths, and that is where I learn to give myself to you."

CHOICE: "I am committing myself to you in spite of all that could happen to me because I believe in you."

In the process of discernment concerning your prayer, a good criterion at the beginning is to check if it is set on the register of *affection*. We will see shortly that we will have to consider delicate shades of meaning. But for the time being:

Do I try to maintain a small dose of warmth in my relationship with the Beloved?

Do I strive to overcome my natural torpor and indifference when I am with him?

In the tools I use, words, glances, gestures, do I incorporate a small measure of affection so that my heart may lean towards him? Or is it only mechanical?

I dare hope that the ways of prayer that we have explored in the previous chapters take on all their meaning here.

Do not neglect the atmosphere and the environment. For our two lovers, candles, floral arrangements, soft music, diffused lighting and even the layout of the tableware, all that had a role to play.

Without going as far as that, do I choose the right place, organizing a special décor in a corner of the room if necessary? Another lighting arrangement? Perhaps a candle? Do I move away from noise, from the telephone?

If you choose to sit in the chair at your desk for your half-hour of meditation, you know what will happen as well as I do …

While you are about it, ask yourself at what time of the day you are most easily touched by a landscape, a poem, music. For some, this will be in the morning. For those, it would be advisable to set their prayer at that time, because it is also then that God will have a greater chance of "touching" them. For others, including myself, it will be in the evening. In the morning I am as cold as marble. Take advantage of this time to tell me off. I will not react. Guaranteed. By that same fact, I pray in a profitable manner especially in the evening.

Therefore, do whatever you can to set your prayer on the register of the *affective* zone. But, unfortunately, this is not an absolute criterion. You may have made the effort to put warmth into it, without succeeding for all that. We are not masters of our *affective* zone as much as we would like to be. Worse still, as you make progress in the ways of contemplative prayer, you will have more and more the *impression* that your mental prayer is becoming arid. Note that this may be the case. But most of the time, this is due to the fact that *the affectivity is becoming more and more restrained* in its subjective manifestations.

We could compare this with the graphic pattern of a cardiogram. In the first phase of your journey, the oscillations, as much upwards as downwards, are important. As a rule, this coincides with the conversation-prayer. "Lord, I praise you for all things." A high point. "Lord, I have nothing to tell you." A low point. And so on. Then, with time, the fluctuations decrease. Henceforth, a word, a glance or a gesture is enough to arouse a small glow of fervor for God. Everything benefits from moderation. What your tenderness for God gains in continuity, it loses in amplitude. If the contact seems easier to maintain, the ascents as well as the descents are not so pronounced. With the passage of time, the process loses more and more of its luster. The oscillations are no longer anything but light fluctuations: a slight touch of the prayer-word or a vague beginning of a gesture is enough to keep your attachment to God awake. The invocation becomes more and more evanescent, seems almost imperceptible. Basic repetition would now appear to be superfluous. It is almost a distraction.

And, logically, you have at the same time the impression that you love no more: you no longer do anything or say anything and almost no longer feel anything. You have the impression that the feeling of love for God is diminished to the point of being almost totally extinguished. This is quite disturbing. If you question yourself, you have to answer, "Yes, I think that God is there, but ..." More than ever, remember then that the Lord is not an object of pleasure for the senses, even if at times he makes his presence felt. More often, you will experience only an inner certitude devoid of all feelings or sensations. Having reached this stage, Bossuet spoke of a "non-felt feeling" of his presence. Other mystics used the image of an ember. It is no longer a fire with flames going up and down, it is no longer anything but a tiny pile of glowing coals. Blowing on it, going back to repetition, would put it out. Gently breathing on it to keep the soul warm is enough.

So, if you go back literally to the criterion mentioned above, "the greater the affection, the better," you will breathe on it with full capacity … and jeopardize everything. You will be tempted to go back to tricks of prayer that worked in the past, and go against the ways of the Spirit. The latter invariably arranges things so that you take up less and less space, and he, more and more. The challenge is to let him have his way. To blow less and less on the flame. "There is no mental prayer in which 'nothing is done' and in which 'nothing happens,' even if there may exist a prayer where nothing is seen, felt or thought."[5]

In short, because of these two reasons (on the one hand, you are not entirely in control of the warmth of your *affective* zone and, on the other, the *affective* zone seems more and more lukewarm as you progress), assessing your prayer solely by this thermometer would be hazardous.

Yet, this whole discussion will not have been useless. If it does not allow you to cast a judgment on your prayer, if it lets you know what you must try to do at all times to achieve it. *Affectionizing.* This is a neologism, but allow me to use it. *Affectionizing.* You must work in this direction during your mental prayer, direct your loving ingenuity. Here I am not recommending affectation or sentimentality. It is not a matter of confusing prayer with the emotional resonance that may accompany it. There remains the fact that if love consists in a mutual gift of self, you must, as you know, be able to express it.

You must apply yourself to express it. Often also without success, alas.

"Do I talk too much (or not enough) when I pray?"

"That has no importance. If words come to you, express your faith and your heart. If not, let it go."

"But my hour of prayer is a tissue of distractions …"

We will have to speak of this at greater length. But I may tell you already that the best remedy is to nourish your affection for him. I, too, believed for many years that the main struggle in prayer was fighting off distractions. To the extent that I had started up a file entitled "Anti-distraction devices." After trying them out, I would evaluate each one on a scale of one to ten, in their order of effectiveness. This is telling you that I was taking this battle to heart. Already, the whole thing was taking on airs of a worldwide conflict, when I became aware that it was better to make peace. In any case, I was always beaten. With the help of experience, I believe more and more now that the main stakes of prayer do not consist in fighting off distractions that are its parasites, but to make it warmhearted. If your prayer is warmhearted, you will not have distractions. Like two lovers whom nothing disturbs. Or rather, they will be like white clouds moving across a blue sky. They are really there. We see them go by. But we have no urge to venture out against them; we feel so good with him.

— Am I using the right word, the right gesture?

— That is not the question. Do not try to change. Only seek to put in a little tenderness.

— Is the tempo too rapid, too slow? Must I concentrate more on the content? Is my silence long enough?

— Do not ask yourself so many questions. One sole thing is important: to try, *if possible,* to keep your relationship with God on the level of *affection.*

A Prayer in the Secondary Registers

It sometimes happens that prayer comes together on the first keyboard, that of *pleasure*. Especially in the beginning.

PLEASURE: "Lord, meeting you gives me an intense joy that resonates in my whole being."

AFFECTION: "I have not yet learned to lean on you on my good as on my bad days."

CHOICE: "I do not see the necessity of committing myself faithfully to you."

A prayer totally centered on consolations. A prayer moved by the fresh experience of a conversion: that of last Wednesday. A prayer limited to the famous long-awaited weekly evenings of communal prayer.

So much the better if that sustains you and draws you nearer to the Lord. "Take advantage of it while it lasts," as we say. Because the day will come when the Spirit will turn off the tap. If by then, you have not developed a deeper relationship with the Lord on the level of a mutual communication through spiritual reading, Scripture study and the reception of the sacraments, you will not be able to keep it up when the season of Alleluias disappears. And if you do not choose the commitment of fidelity, you will not be able to cross the inevitable deserts.

In short, I will say no more here than what the whole spiritual tradition teaches us about this delectable prayer: "Take advantage of the time now to gather provisions in your storehouse, you will need them when the days of famine come." We could say that the discernment you would need to make in this case would be of a preventive order: presuming as early as now the end of the heavenly dew.

Alas, the fate of the routine pray-ers that we have become, or that we will become, is more deplorable. Exactly the opposite of the previous case: there remains more or less only a dried-up fidelity, a perseverance that is totally bare before God.

PLEASURE: "I have no longer felt anything for a long time."

AFFECTION: "I feel empty when I have to speak to you."

CHOICE: **"I cling to it because in spite of everything I believe in it."**

You recognize yourself? Unfortunate, is it not? If prayer played on the *affective register* is "normal" in the sense that it should serve as a norm and model, the one which limits itself to choice is also "normal": it corresponds to the most frequent type of prayer and is the lot of the greatest number.

So how should such a prayer be assessed? I can hear you grumbling already:

"It is packed full of distractions, one has hardly left me when two others come along. Is this serious, doctor? No feelings of affection … nothing ever happens … wasted time. A bad sign, is it not? God seems to be so far, so very far from me … Repeated failures Catastrophic, no?"

And adding with an air of despair:

"I can struggle all I want, impossible to change anything. I am doomed from the start." If this is your case, I suggest that you reshuffle your cards and go over the rules of the game.

Would not the first criterion to use in measuring the worth of your prayer be the *time you devote to it*? Madeleine Delbrêl, whom we have mentioned already, defined prayer as "setting aside some time the sole purpose of which is to be offered to God."[6] Nothing else. The first law of prayer is to endure, to hold on, to cling to it, to exhaust the time allotted to it. So to evaluate it, you must ask yourself:

"*Have I devoted the necessary time to it?* Did I plan my day's schedule accordingly? Except for a major reason, did I abide by it? Did I put in the time right to the end of the period?"

The first quality of prayer will never be its sublime nature, its loftiness, its cleverness, but only its fidelity. Remember the Gospel: Jesus insists on nothing but perseverance. Which simply means repetition and quantity that may be measured on a watch. He warns us against nothing but losing heart: the main obstacle, the only temptation.

I share my deepest conviction with you. No better proof of our love for God then to devote to him the irreplaceable hour of our life that is passing by. And this will be all the truer if this hour offered to him is a libation strictly of no profit to us. Then we are giving him our very being. What are we indeed if not time flowing on from the moment of our birth to that of our death? And then we are sacrificing to him but one slice of it. To him alone. With no return for ourselves, even if we ponder over it.

> Let us give it [this period of time] to him freely, with our minds unoccupied by other things and entirely resolved never to take it back again, whatever we may suffer through trials, annoyances or aridities. Let me realize that this time

is being lent me, and is not my own, and feel that I can rightly be called to account for it if I am not prepared to devote it wholly to God.[7]

For lack of quality, give him quantity. God is not looking for people who pray well, but for people who pray much. The less you pray, the less you will feel like praying. Even if the little that remains seems of quality to you. The more you pray, the more you will feel like praying. To the point of no longer being able to go without doing so. Even if you have the impression of not knowing how to go about doing this.

As a second criterion, should you not consider the *care you take to start off your session of prayer really well*? I agree that you are not in control of what happens (or does not happen) once your ship is launched, but you can always *hoist up the sails*. Then … let God take care of the rest. The Curé of Ars said that a poorly prepared prayer is a prayer poorly made. So, so much more so, a poorly committed prayer. Therefore, the second question to evaluate it becomes:

"*Was I careful to start it well?* Were the conditions of place and time favorable? Did I break away completely from my tasks? Was I consciously aware of the presence of God?"

This is the easiest moment since you are still all new. You board the ship and you still have the helm in hand.

If you enter into your period of prayer while the television is still on … Or if you have a look at your computer before starting your prayer in case you have received some e-mail. To be read later, of course …

You may have to go through the process of beginning several times while you are on your way. No matter. Total loss of direction in the storm? Start over very humbly as if you were setting up the sails again.

The third and last criterion is the *management of your distractions*. You will have some. Guaranteed. The question to ask is not at all:

"Am I guilty of having some?"

It would be rather:

"What did I do when I became aware of them?"

You may already have wandered for three or four minutes before you become aware of them. Nothing is wrong until now. But then, what did you do? This is the crucial point. Did you put aside this distraction radically to come back to God? Or did you keep on wandering about because this was more interesting?

You have the extraordinary chance of proving to God that you prefer him to the distraction. So then, a distraction is formidable! Every time it comes, it provides you the opportunity to manifest your love to God, not in an abstract way made up of good intentions, but in a real, measurable way on *terra firma*.

"Lord, I choose to re-pray. I prefer you rather than this flitting about that is nonetheless so alluring. My distractions are always more interesting than you are, Lord, but you are the one I am choosing."

Besides, if this preference is accompanied by the feeling of humility for having "reached only this point" and by the desire to come out of it, therefore to do better next time, do not have any qualms of conscience, you are a winner.

On some days you will have up to five hundred distractions an hour, apparently the average number for a normal person. Well, you will have the opportunity of witnessing five hundred times to your attachment to God. What luck!

I admit that I was tempted to entitle this paragraph: "In praise of distracted prayer." I would have concluded by saying: "Have as many distractions as possible, since it is by rejecting them that you will show most love. Each distraction becomes an astonishing grace. Thank God every time you have the privilege of rejecting one."

In short, prayer is assured uniquely according to these three criteria: the time devoted to it faithfully, the effort to make a good beginning, the choice made at the time of distractions. And never according to what I have experienced or felt. Or did not feel. Therefore according to *my free giving* and not according to *the results*.

During her annual retreat, a sister of adoration asked to see me. According to the rules of her community, she had to make an hour of adoration every day before the Blessed Sacrament exposed. Straightaway, she complained with anguish that all she does is sleep during this time. To relieve the tension of the atmosphere a bit, I slipped in this comment with a touch of humor:

"That must be restful for you…"

"On the contrary, I come out of there utterly exhausted."

But then everything becomes clear. Her love for God is intact. It is even a struggle and a frantic battle. Is this not an amazing prayer? And which, over and above all, keeps her in humility …

A Prayer in the Wrong Registers

It may happen that the situation is more delicate, and this is notably the case when prayer is focused on components that while being part of the human being are outside the proper domain of love.

SENSIBILITY: "I consider that I am praying when I am deeply moved by the presence of God."

PLEASURE:

AFFECTION:

CHOICE:

IMAGINATION: "I consider that I am praying when my attention remains unfailingly focused on God."

MEMORY: "I consider that I am praying when I repeat carefully the formulas learned by heart."

INTELLIGENCE: "I consider that I am praying when I think of God and reflect on his attributes."

Sensibility

Let us begin with the case of prayer focused on *sensibility*. I was going to say "on *sentimentalism*." I have already pointed this out on several occasions and I am taking advantage of this one to drive the matter home: prayer is not a matter of sensibility. Love is accompanied by feelings – and so is prayer – but love is not a feeling – and neither is prayer. Both have their source in a deeper faculty of the human being.

Up to a certain point, loving is a decision one makes. Thus two persons who get married *mutually promise* to give love to each other. A day will come when in the eyes of the married man, for example, the office secretary will seem more exhilarating than his wife. His *sensibility* will then suggest to him other possible avenues. But his love will take the direction that he will have to choose on an altogether different level: fidelity to his commitment or a new adventure.

Jesus goes so far as to *command* us to love one another. He does not ask us to have overflowing positive impulses of *sensibility* for all those around us, something that would be practical, but impossible. He demands that we behave in a certain way towards them. When we enter into a relationship with others – or when we pray – we are not totally in control of our emotions. The latter arise (or do not arise) without our being fully responsible. Nor fully guilty. In the case of charity, we must try to disregard our natural sympathies or antagonisms. These are real, but belong to *sensibility*. The Gospel is more radical; it asks us to try to do good to those with whom we are in a relationship. This kindliness arises from an organ that is more fundamental than *sensibility* alone. In the case of prayer, we must persevere. We must remain faithful in the absence of attraction. We are touching upon a great truth: we are there for him and not for ourselves.

Thus prayer is not judged according to emotions for it is not identified with these. This does not mean that we must fight them off if they come. Ultimately, does not the recourse to the level of *sensibility* remain ambiguous? How can we kindle feelings in a way that would not be artificial? How could we make repentance, love or gratitude spring up without this area buried in our deepest self being touched and turned about, this area where God can reveal himself: *the depths of the heart*.

Imagination

Some consider prayer, all or parts of it, as a control of the *imagination*. The stakes would then consist in this warfare waged against the enemy we have already met: distractions. Indeed, who has no reason to complain about these parasites? All the more so given that when one of them, more enticing than the others, has filtered into the *mental*, it inevitably lets its essence flow into the *affective*. To hell with silent recollections!

How we can waste energy and ingenuity in controlling them! No recipe seems infallible. In fact, none has compelled recognition throughout the history of spirituality. And this is not because no one has ever tried …

I love this story about a young Jew who goes to see his rabbi and asks him:

"Tell me, Rabbi Moshé, I am thinking of becoming a disciple of Rabbi Isaac so that he may teach me to serve the Most High. But how can one know if the Wisdom of the Lord is with him?"

"Ask him for a trick to chase away distractions. If he gives you one and claims that it is effective, he is a charlatan, let him go."

And yet, if they appear to us as unacceptable sins, what is surprising is that Jesus never demanded that our intimacy with the Father be without distractions. We may even suppose that he himself had some, since he was fully human and that, by this fact, he had the gift of an imagination which, at times, must have played dirty tricks on him.

For lack of better means, I have suggested throughout this book that you use this faculty, representing the Lord to yourself, starting with familiar images with the purpose of being referred back to the essential organ: the *heart*. This is the purpose of the images of liturgy and sacred art.

At the end of it, do not be too upset nor discredit your prayer too much if your imagination wanders. The basic resolution is what must be considered as the rule of assessment.

"I was carried away by my fantasy, of which I am not fully the master, by my dreaming which is flighty. My desire to be God's has remained intact, nonetheless. I know that because I have come back to him regularly."

True prayer is not an unfailing attention but the firm will to belong to him evermore.

Memory

Let us cast a quick glance at another possible situation: at prayer placed in the register of *memory*. Here, the text is known by heart and all we must do is to recite it without putting in too much effort. Practically, if not theoretically, such a prayer could unfold itself outside the area of love, since *memory* has nothing to do with love. No need to love: putting the prayer wheel in action is enough.[8] In the Christian world, the rosary especially has inherited this eccentricity, the breviary as well, even the liturgy of the Eucharist. If the heart is not in it, in vain is the deed.

Since this is no longer in style, and you all agree with me when I say that running off formulas is not praying,[9] I shall move on.

Intelligence

Putting prayer on the level of *intelligence*. A very frequent error. Making it into a cerebral activity. "Place yourself in the presence of God," we are told. Very well. And we sit bolt upright in our chair, back very rigid, head and feet in the proper position, and then we try to *think of nothing.* The more we succeed, the better we sleep.

But when we meet an old friend, we do not sit in front of him, in a Sphinx-like attitude, concentrating sufficiently on him so as not to have any distractions. We speak to each other, smile at each other, pat each other on the back … Why not the same with God?

Ask for some advice on your mental prayer from a "Reverend Father," and he will always be in line with the Sphinx: "Arms well placed, legs in the lotus position," he will tell you, and especially "concentrate yourself." I do not know where this nonsense was picked up but we do not love in that way. And the more you observe these instructions scrupulously, the more you will come to a twofold result: tingling in your legs and a more or less loud snore. No doubt the Reverend Father will add, "Think of God and of his mysteries." Like a lover telling his fiancée:

"Dearest, sit in this corner, as straight and rigid as possible, and then *think of me.*"

When we are in love, we gaze at each other eye to eye, we speak to each other gently, hold hands and hug each other …

We had the misfortune of speaking about "*mental* prayer." But prayer is not made first of all in the head; it is made in the heart of the person, at the full center. That is where the urge to smile at someone begins. That is where the urge to hug is born. That is where the impression of feeling good in the presence of a friend is experienced.

That is where the heartrending is felt when we are betrayed by the lack of fidelity of a partner.

It is also there that prayer must be set.

Father Matteo, a famous popular preacher of two or three generations ago, said, "We are made for prayer. Just the head is superfluous."

He agreed with what the startzi say: "The head is a flea market encumbered by the multitude. One cannot pray to God in this place."[10]

This is not done in contempt for or to humiliate the *intelligence* searching for God.

> We are not here in the myth of the "good savage," of the "blissful imbecile" or of the "enlightened ignoramus." We are simply exploring a space in ourselves beyond all conceptual or imaginary modes. Far from disappearing, the intellect must move down into the heart.[11]

Since this is about reflecting on God, the interplay of concepts is of some use. We compare a concept like the one of power with realities more familiar to us. However, we end up being weary of them. In fact, are arguments able to quench our thirst for God? Do we get in touch with God by making efforts of this kind? It often seems that we do not. At first, perhaps, but very soon the head does not seem to be the best organ to lead us to an encounter with God.[12]

> To descend into our hearts, it is proper to bring other more interior, more mysterious and more hidden faculties into play. Our reasoning intelligence must stop discoursing to let us discover another space, so much more gratifying.[13]

God awaits us there with an infinite patience.

Notes

[1] Yves de Montcheuil, *Problèmes de vie spirituelle* (Paris: Épi, 1963), p. 80.

[2] In this section, I am drawing from Yves Saint-Arnaud, *J'aime* (Montreal: Éditions de l'Homme, 1978).

[3] The three components dealt with here correspond quite well to the three forms of love that certain Greek thinkers called *Eros*, *Philia* and *Agape*.

[4] Therapists teach to begin statements with "I" instead of "You." Not to say, "*You* always come late for supper…" but "I feel frustrated when you are not on time for supper…"

[5] Thomas Merton, *Les chemins de la joie* (Paris: Plon, 1961), p. 53.

[6] Madeleine Delbrêl, *La joie de croire* (Paris: Seuil, 1967), p. 203.

[7] *The Complete Works of Saint Teresa of Jesus*, vol. 2, *Way of perfection*, p. 98.

[8] The prayer wheel is a sacred instrument of the Tibetans. It is made of a hollow metal cylinder that turns on an axle, in which are enclosed slips of paper or fabric covered with prayers. Every time it is turned from right to left (the rotation in the opposite direction destroys the effectiveness of the act), we acquire the same merits as if we had read what is written inside it from beginning to end. Similar instruments have been found in Assyria and Persia.

[9] A frequent confusion arises from placing forgiveness in the area of memory.
"I would like to forgive but I cannot manage to forget."
"Congratulations. This is a sign that you have an excellent memory. Fortunately, forgiveness is something else."

In fact, forgiveness is an *act of love*, considered for the sake of certain values, and therefore placed in the register of *choice*. It does not consist of forgetting; besides, how could we still forgive what we do not remember? We can forgive only what we have not managed to forget. Forgiveness consists in not making the other pay for the injury done to us. It is a decision and a *choice* we make. Ideally, and here is what becomes difficult, forgiveness would have to include with time the area of the *affective* (that bonds of sharing be rewoven with the offender). And the summit will be nonetheless when the domain of *pleasure* is converted (when resentment disappears and meeting the offender again becomes a pleasant moment).
The Risen Christ did not forget his passion; on the contrary, he shows his wounds to his disciples. But instead of making them pay for their betrayal, he makes of it precisely the very instrument of their salvation.
Ah! If I could transform injuries into opportunities of doing good to my enemies …

[10] Theophane the Recluse, quoted in Igumen Chariton of Valaam, *op. cit.,* p. 252.

[11] Daniel Maurin, *op. cit.,* p. 109.

[12] Sometimes we also make the mistake of putting forgiveness on the level of the intelligence. At the cost of a distortion of the latter: "No, what you did to me is not serious." Or, "It's nothing, it did not hurt me." Or again, "It was not your fault."
We then confuse forgiveness and excuses, even forgiveness and denial of facts. These notions may sometimes overlap, but when there is a true offence, forgiveness amounts to saying (and to doing):
"What you did was wrong. It made me suffer. It was deliberate on your part. But I decided not to take revenge. To act in such a way that this wrong be not an obstacle to our relationships."

[13] Daniel Maurin, *op. cit.,* p. 41.

Epilogue

"Love always makes
those eloquent that have it."[1]
Christopher Marlowe

Since then, the animals have dispersed. But because of the mistake in the beginning, a spokesperson had to be designated again. This is always so. We must say that the apple story that followed fixed nothing.

Be careful not to make the Monkey dwelling in us talk too much. His tirades give us a good conscience, but he is not aware of the fact that the Pink Flamingo sleeps standing on its foot.

Easy for us not to choose the Peacock. Relatively easy not to make the Giraffe speak.

We are more tempted to vote for the Finch in us. We think that love must be sung. In this case, he would be such a good ambassador. When we think that love is an emotion, we tend to thrust out our breast.

The problem with the Dove is that it is terribly timid. It moans only when the others are quiet. Not being much inclined to change his mind, God's choice seems to hold in spite of all. His Spirit, the perfect Dove, intercedes in us with “sighs too deep for words” (*Rom* 8:26).

Praying is … managing to force the other animals to be quiet.

Praying would be … making those two Doves moan in unison.

[1] Christopher Marlowe, *Hero and Leander (1598)*, ed. Millar Maclure (London: Methuen & Co. Ltd., 1968), Sestiad 2, line 72, p. 30.

For Further Reflection

MAURIN, Daniel, *Seven Lessons on the Prayer of the Heart* (Montreal: Médiaspaul, 1996). Highly recommended.

TERESA OF AVILA, *Way to Perfection* in *The Complete Works of Saint Teresa of Jesus,* trans. and ed. by Allison Peers, 3 vols. (London: Sheed & Ward, 1946), vol. 2. A work that cannot be ignored which, in spite of centuries, is easy to read. Written with the breath of holiness.

KEATING, Thomas, O.C.S.O. (with B. Pennington and T. Clarke), *Finding Grace at the Center* (Petersham, Massachusetts: St. Bede Publications, 1978). *The Heart of the World: An Introduction to Contemplative Christianity* (New York: Crossroads, 1981). *Open Mind, Open Heart* (New York: Amity House, 1986). Practical presentation of the centering prayer. Easy approach.

MAIN, John, O.S.B., *Christian Meditation: The Gethsemane Talks* (Tucson: Medio Media, 1985). *Word into Silence* (Continuum: New York, 1998). Very easy to read.

PENNINGTON, Basil, O.C.S.O., *Centering Prayer: Renewing an Ancient Christian Prayer Form* (New York: Doubleday, 1980). *Daily We Touch Him: Practical Religious Experiences* (New York: Image Books, 1979). *Centered Living* (New York: Image Books, 1986). *Call to the Center* (New York: Doubleday Image Books, 1990). Always easy, with a pedagogical flair. The centering prayer is closer to my ideas about the prayer-word of the School of Christian Meditation.

Ratzinger, Joseph, *Christian Meditation: Letter on Some Aspects of Christian Meditation* (Montreal: Médiaspaul, 1990), pp. 16-23. To be consulted on discernment.

Achevé d'imprimer
en mai 2001
sur les presses de
Imprimerie H.L.N.

Imprimé au Canada – Printed in Canada